Lighting the Stage

A Lighting Designer's Experiences

Lighting the Stage

A Lighting Designer's Experiences

by Francis Reid

(f)

Focal Press
An imprint Butterworth-Heinemann Ltd
Linacre House, Jordan Hill, Oxford OX2 8DP

ℛ A member of the Reed Elsevier plc group

OXFORD   LONDON   BOSTON
MUNICH   NEW DELHI   SINGAPORE   SYDNEY
TOKYO   TORONTO   WELLINGTON

First published 1995
Reprinted 1995

Text © Francis Reid 1995
Illustrations © Sarah Ward 1995

British Library Cataloguing in Publication Data
A CIP record for this book is available from the British Library

Library of Congress Cataloging in Publication Data
A catalogue record for this book is available on request

ISBN 0 240 51375 4

Printed and bound in Great Britain by Clays Ltd, St Ives plc

Contents

Preface

Most books about stage lighting tend to concentrate on the factual aspects of equipment and the design process. This book acknowledges that theatre is essentially a *people* industry and is an attempt to discuss some of the relationships involved in lighting design. Relationships between the people involved and between these people and the technology used in the course of applying their craft. Who are these lighting designers? What makes them tick? Where do they slot into the creative team? What are their priorities? How do they learn to light? What are the fears, agonies and ecstasies of this little corner of the theatre industry?

Lighting design is low on objective facts and high on debatable opinions. Much of a lighting designer's thinking tends to be lateral – intuitive rather than logical. So, inevitably, the book is written from a highly personal viewpoint. Its 'thinking aloud' approach is one which I have used in magazine essays over the past 25 years and I have been encouraged by the response of lighting designers, technicians and students. Indeed, anyone familiar with my magazine writings, particularly in *Tabs* and *Cue*, now both, sadly, deceased, may recognise some reworking of earlier attempts to explain the mysteries of lighting design.

I have avoided the equipment photographs which traditionally illustrate lighting books. In this instance, they would be in the nature of graffiti, distracting from, rather than supporting, the book's argument. Likewise, there are no production photographs: even if emulsion responded to contrast in the same way as the human eye, stage lighting is so dynamic that moments of frozen stillness have little significance.

Francis Reid

Painting The Light

The painting on the cover is a 1977 evocation by Charles Bravery of the author focusing lights for a 1963 production of *Pelleas et Melisande*. The bats are a clue to the identity of the opera house – although the *Glyndebourne* bats of that era normally emerged only for scenes lit in the full romantic-blue of an operatic moon.

Charles Bravery, the master scenic artist of our age, was steeped in the English scene-painting tradition symbolised by the dynasty of the Harkers and it was Charles on the paint frame of the Harker Studios in London's Walworth Road that several decades of leading designers looked to for a creative realisation of their designs. Oliver Messel, John Piper and Osbert Lancaster were just some of the set designers who would consider no other artist to paint their sets.

Charles was one of my great teachers. I visited his paint frame and he came to my lighting rehearsals. I would light into his paint and he would paint into my light. He modified his pigments and I modified my filters. I tried to minimise adverse actor–light interactions on the set and, when my minimum was more than his optimum, he darkened and textured the surface to restore it to the quality of the set designer's model. For me, it was a wonderful learning experience about the interaction between paint and light. But he turned my learning into a collaboration for, like any great teacher, he respected the embryonic artistry of his pupil.

Beni Montressor designed the sets and costumes for this *Pelleas* and the director was Carl Ebert – another sympathetic teacher who walked with his lighting designer among the forest gauzes explaining the significance of light in the original poem of *Maeterlinck*, and Debussy's musical response to it. The first night of *Pelleas* was one of the great moments of my life. The conductor, Vittorio Gui, sitting by the prompt-corner awaiting his call to the pit, beckoned me over: "Francis," he confided, "I worked with

Debussy and I know what he wanted for his opera. Tonight we are giving it to him." He went on to say nice things about the interaction of the music and the light, but it was his word 'we' that gave me my real high. His inflexion on 'we' acknowledged that the light was integrated into the work of the entire production team. As I floated away, my thoughts were for Charles Bravery because I know that light means absolutely nothing until it hits something.

1
Being a
Lighting
Designer

Designed light is not a new phenomenon, but specialist lighting designers are. Performances have always involved decisions about light. The earliest outdoor rituals were positioned to take optimum advantage of natural light and early theatre buildings were sited with regard to the trajectory of the sun. Since the very first indoor theatres, the positioning of every lamp – whether candle, oil, gas or electric – has involved a design decision. Just as there has always been designed light, there have always been people responsible for designing that light. They may not have been called lighting designer but they were always there, making design decisions, usually as one of many duties in a combined role. However, the second-half of our century has seen the emergence of a specialist who assumes design responsibilities, within the creative team, for the lighting.

Why have a specialist person to make the lighting decisions? Why not the director? Or the scene designer? Or a joint operation by the pair of them? The need for a specialist arises partly out of the size of the workload and partly from a general desire to develop the role of light by taking advantage of new possibilities offered by rapidly-advancing technology. Lighting has become a bigger operation as we have sought to do more with light by using equipment installations which have become larger and increasingly complex. The history books are full of theatre workers whose lighting ambitions far exceeded the technology available to them. But the situation today is reversed: any failure of the light to support a stage production is more likely to arise from a lack of corporate imagination and organisation by the production team than from any deficiencies in the available technology.

Directing was once a much simpler matter. Many of the directors of my youth were really just traffic police. They spent little time discussing motivation and they would have been somewhat baffled by the philosophers and psychotherapists who inhabit today's rehearsal rooms. Scenery is no longer a merely decorative background: the set designer provides a stage environment which supports the actors and seeks to offer a visual metaphor for the text. Director and designer are just too busy with their own work to be able to give proper attention to the details of light. It is a classic case of the need for a division of labour.

Apart from sharing the workload, there is also a need for someone to concentrate on maximising the contribution of light. Nothing in this world ever behaves exactly as we would wish and light is no exception. A degree of compromise is inevitable and should be made by someone who can approach the problem with some possibility of objective neutrality. Apart from individual production team members having different visual priorities, there is one major area in particular where even the wonders of modern technology are defeated by the basic laws of physics. Modern spotlights offer very sophisticated control of light beams, enabling them to be sized, shaped, coloured, textured and hardened or diffused. Everything can be controlled except the length of the beam which just keeps on travelling in a straight line until it hits an actor. It would be marvellous if we could chop off the rest of the beam. But, alas, any light which is not stopped by the actor passes on until it hits the scenery. This can result in difficulties in balancing a light picture to satisfy the ideals of both director and scene designer. There often has to be some compromise – the best compromise can usually be reached by a third person who not only understands the two sides of the problem and is sympathetic to both, but also has the technical knowledge to implement the best compromise.

It is interesting that lighting designers first emerged in the commercial theatres of New York, then spread to London as a means of saving money by getting light into a managed situation. I remember being interviewed by a theatre manager for one of my earliest jobs as a freelance lighting designer.

He said:

"I have had some truly wonderful lighting in my theatre in the past, absolutely wonderful. I have had directors who have made wonderful light and scene designers who have made wonderful light. But they festooned my theatre with lighting equipment and kept my technicians out of bed all night. I expect you – as a specialist lighting designer – to light my show just as well, hopefully even a little better. But, more importantly, you will be able to do it with far fewer spotlights, everybody will get to bed before midnight, and you will save me much more money than I am going to pay you."

The managers of non-commercial theatres quickly picked up on the efficiency angle. Efficiency may not always be the very first thought of such creative idealists as actors, scenographers and directors, but they soon discovered that with a designer the lighting could get better.

Unlike earlier theatrical eras, today's staging has no stock-in-trade solutions and procedures: productions are staged in a very wide range of alternative styles. Every style is possible, none excluded – no matter how surprising some of these styles would seem to Chekhov, Mozart or Shakespeare. The preparation for staging each new interpretation of a dramatic text or music score starts with a search for an appropriate style: acting style, movement style, scenic style, costume style – and lighting style. It is essential to address the question: 'How will we use light in this production?' Someone has to be responsible for debating and integrating the contribution of light. Asking questions, suggesting different possibilities, establishing a consensus and integrating the lighting concept within a team who hold corporate responsibility for the production under the leadership of a director – who holds the ultimate power of veto. But good directors, like good leaders of democratic governments, aim to lead in the spirit of being 'first among equals'. Good directors are hypersensitive to human feelings because they have to be able to draw, perhaps even coax, creativity out of their colleagues. Stage production has become a team activity with the lighting designer an indispensable member of the team.

Stage lighting stands at the crossroads of art and science, yet detailed technical knowledge is not essential. Indeed, there could well be a risk that too much technological background may inhibit imagination rather than stimulate it. For a lighting designer, the science tends to be simpler than the art. Handling the technology is the easy bit: the core skills of a lighting designer are handling ideas and handling people. What do lighting designers 'do'? An accurate, if superficial, description of the role of a lighting designer might be something along the following lines.

Lighting designers take the lead, in conjunction with the rest of the team, in the concept and development of the lighting style. They establish where light is required and where it is not required – its quality, its colour, its quantity. Then they devise a means of implementing this by decisions about where to position lighting instruments, how to focus them, which types of instruments to use, their colour filters, etc. This is a drawing-board process, now being overtaken by computer-based drafting. It is a process which is like an iceberg – the greater proportion is hidden from view, not under the sea but away from the stage.

The lighting designer then supervises all the preparations, in association with colleagues who have technological responsibilities, visiting the rehearsal room as much as possible to absorb the action and continue dis-cussions with the director and other members of the production team. And then he or she implements the design during the technical and dress rehearsals, according to the prepared plan but keeping a flexible approach to possible change and development throughout.

However, this simple statement of fact rather disguises the real personal and group agonising which is at the heart of any creative process.

If there is a danger in being a lighting-person, it is that one might cease to be a total theatre-person: anyone involved in lighting is just a general theatre-person who happens to specialize in light but remains fascinated by, and involved in, the whole business of the stage. Lighting designers are ideas people but, in the spirit of creative teamwork, they do not impose these ideas. Lighting designers are also management people who plan and monitor a complex sequence of resource-intensive procedures involving people and equipment.

I know no greater terror than the sheet of blank paper – whether it is actual sheet of paper or a metaphor for an empty stage – or my empty head. What contribution is light going to make to this production? This question triggers a complex sequence of interacting decisions. Even when the lighting designer has developed a personal vision, will this vision be shared by the rest of the team? Or can it be sold to them? How far, if at all, have director, choreographer and scene designer developed the role of light within their own vision of the production?

The production process is bedevilled by problems of communication – particularly when words have to be used to discuss concepts that are essentially visual. Set and costume designs are scaled pictorial images of what will be seen on stage, whereas a lighting design comprises lists and diagrams which bear no visual relationship to the stage picture. Current experiments confirm the promise that computer simulation will eventually offer visualisation of lit scenes on a video screen: not just as a series of frozen moments but as a dynamically changing cue sequence. But 'eventually' is far enough into tomorrow's world to ensure that verbal uncertainties will continue to remain a feature of lighting design for at least the next decade. Even if there appears to be a clear consensus of lighting aims for the production, there are still hours of design time at the drawing board. Much of this time is devoted to agonising over priorities such as:

- Just how much of the budget can we blow on that big two-minute effect without making the remaining two hours look boringly-bland or just plain underlit?

- How low can I come to get light under the eyebrows and into the eyes without raising intrusive shadows behind the actor?

I don't think that answering questions like these is ever going to be made any easier by some 'magic' software program that sifts through the options and advises you. How we document the design has changed fast. I still use tracing paper, stencils and pens, but I am one of a fast-diminishing breed. If I were younger, I would be knocking on my bank manager's door for help to invest in a major computer-aided design (CAD) system such as *Autocad*. This is definitely an area where the cursor is mightier than the pen. Not just for the clean drawings and the ability to stroke a key which will change the display immediately from plan to section in order to see just how a particular angle of light is going to hit the actor, but for the automatic generation of equipment listings, especially in that area where I frequently miscount — the colour call. But there is a danger: computer-aided design programs have the ability to generate so much paper, so easily, there is a possibility we might swamp ourselves and our colleagues with lists of doubtful value.

There has always been a danger of generating too much paper. A lighting design is a very insubstantial piece of work until it is realised on the stage. Because the graphics of the plan are just diagrams which bear no relation to what the lit stage will actually look like, there is a temptation to give the design an impression of importance by increasing the amount of paperwork. I hope that CAD will help to save the rainforests rather than turn even more trees into lists of questionable value.

Throughout the preparation before, and during, the period in the rehearsal room, the lighting designer has to live with self-doubt. Is the vision in my head correct for the play? Although this vision does seem to be shared by the rest of the team, are we all really talking about the same thing? Am I responding to the way the production is developing in rehearsal? Will my lighting rig offer a sufficiently flexible palette? As the move from rehearsal room to stage approaches, the anxiety curve shifts ever closer to the vertical...

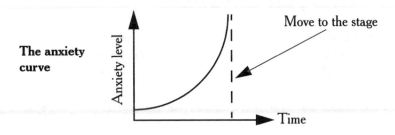

As I watch the final run-throughs, I am only too aware that lighting remains the one intangible in the production. Nobody, not even me, has seen anything of the lighting. Scenery fit-up and instrument focusing are times of deep concentration – adapting to surprises and repairing miscalculations while keeping the broad outline of the original vision clearly in view. The most difficult cue in any show is the first one. The most stomach-wrenching moment for any lighting designer is the walk from stage to auditorium after focusing. All these lights so carefully planned, rigged, coloured and delicately tweaked. A moment of silence: realising that we have finished trying to communicate with electricians at the tops of ladders, piano tuners suddenly cease twanging, carpenters switch off their power tools and stage managers stop asking "I don't want to hurry you, and I know you started late because the scenery was not ready, but can you give me some idea of when focusing is likely to finish?"

Now it is finished and as we make our way to the production desk in the auditorium, we have but one thought: will all those individual beams add up to anything? At the most basic, will there be seamless joins or will it be like a colander with actors standing in black holes? Plus more agony about all the discussions we had with the director, choreographer, set and costume designers. Discussions when we tried to find words to describe visual things. Did we all mean the same thing? During this walk from stage to auditorium all the uncertainties of the weeks of preparation flash through the mind, just like the life review that is said to accompany drowning.

I put the cans on, mutter a few nervous pleasantries to the board operator, and go into my old up-a-point\down-a-point routine – my antennae twitching for a favourable sound from the rest of the team gathered around me. Occasionally I sense an appreciative murmur, even a whispered "Nice!" – but more often there is just that ominous silence which passes for concentration. I try to interpret any 'grunts' and 'hmms' as I move towards the moment when I offer up cue one – "How does this sort of thing grab you?" I enquire with studied nonchalance – as if it were work in progress, leaving myself room to manoeuvre although I am hoping that, basically, this is it. With any luck, one might hear "Y–eee–s, fine." – perhaps tempered with "Do you think we have enough light for the actors down left?" – from the director, or "I wonder how the sky would look with just a touch more green–blue at the bottom?" – from the set designer. After the first few cues it usually becomes easier – our nagging fears were unfounded. The palette is working. We can start to motor, perhaps even enjoy some brief moments of satisfaction. There will always be surprises. The way that a light strikes an element of scenery often triggers ideas – not just in the head of the lighting designer but in those of the director, choreographer and other members of the design team. Lighting designers must stand ready to respond to their own ideas and to those of the rest of the team – being flexible but alert to measuring new details against the total concept.

When working as a lighting designer, my normal wish for is more *time*. Time to hang some extra lights, and time to focus them. Time to experiment. Time to make mistakes. Time to take risks and time to go back to the old safe solution if the risky idea does not work out. Remember the daily prayer of every theatre worker:

"Please give me the right to fail, but please do not let it happen too often."

Time on a stage is very expensive, especially lighting time when so many other people have to stand around waiting for the light-people to do their thing. But time is not only expensive, it is often in such short supply that it cannot be bought: the opening night is fixed and the tickets are sold. All we can do is to carefully plan ahead for all routine matters so that no crucial creative stage-time is lost whilst dealing with factual technical difficulties which could have been foreseen.

Lighting designers try to avoid saying "No!" Instead, they sound just a little doubtful as they indicate half-hearted agreement while laying out the consequences of following through on any proposal they do not feel comfortable with. They keep their cool. If the board operator hits the wrong button and loses a memorised cue, lighting designers do not scream but quietly make the cue again, consoling themselves by knowing that it may well look better at a second attempt.

The board operator is, of course, one of the two really key production people in a lighting designer's life. The actual lighting boards do not matter much. What really matters is whether operators *like their board*. If they do, they can make it do anything. I find that the more an operator likes a board, the less likely it is to break down. Accuracy, sensitivity and keeping cool are the operator skills that comfort a lighting designer. The other key person is the stage manager who gives the cues ('calls the show') – normally the Deputy Stage Manager in British theatre. A good show-caller is sensitive to each performance's subtly-different timing, resulting from the interaction between actor and each day's audience. The subtle differences that make live-theatre, live! Also important is the way that these cues are called – a calm, confident voice on the cans does wonders to keep paranoia at bay – the paranoia that hovers just under the surface of every technical rehearsal, dress rehearsal and first performance.

One area where the whole production in general, but the lighting designer in particular, is totally dependent upon people is *follow-spotting*. The 'Limes', as I still like to call my follow-spot operators, really do have the potential to mess up the show. Our dependence on people quality here is particularly acute because, when the Limes get it wrong, the audience notice, whereas in some other areas of stage technology only the technicians are aware that something is not as it should be.

Lighting designers need to be sensitive to actors' understandable fear of technology. The show develops delicately in the rehearsal room until it is a finely-honed piece of ensemble acting, played to a small production team sitting at a table against the wall. It took weeks to get it to this pitch. Then, suddenly, it is pitchforked on to the stage with only a few days to integrate with a hi-tech environment. The actors come on stage. They look out front. In the centre of the great, dark auditorium void there is a formidable array of technology that looks increasingly like mission control. Banks of computer screens. Shadowy figures wearing cans and chanting. Who can blame the actors for feeling that their performances are about to be taken over?

All theatre workers are obsessive about their own specialist area and lighting designers are no exception. Yet light is such an integral part of the whole production that they must cultivate the ability to take a wide overview. The nature of the job requires them to be communicators. Indeed, the width of their necessary understanding of the theatre process, together with their need to communicate and be sensitive to human psychology, has resulted in many lighting designers becoming consultants and administrators of all kinds. Survival in lighting requires the acquisition of what has become fashionably known as *transferable skills*. There is no shortage of lighting designers so material wealth tends to be elusive, while the working hours play havoc with any planned social life. Statistics indicate that major hazards of the job include alcoholism and divorce. But none of this has ever been known to deter anyone who is determined to design light.

Life in the theatre spans agony and ecstasy. The quest for perfection requires a lot of self-assessment and that, inevitably, includes self-doubt. But there are rewards. Such as one of the highlights, perhaps the climax, of my career. We had finished a dress rehearsal and adjourned for notes. It was a civilised theatre company so these notes were given in the bar. The director went round with his spiral-topped notebook. It was a long session involving deep individual discussions with each of the actors in turn. Finally he got to me, flicked over the pages with furrowed brow and then said, apologetically, "Francis, I'm terribly terribly sorry, but I didn't notice the lighting tonight." What more could I have wished for!

Lighting ideal...

One fine day, I was assisting with the education of tomorrow's technicians. "At what point," I enquired, "should the lighting designer become involved in the planning of a new production?" Quick as a flash came the reply from a likely lad "As soon as he has signed his contract." The same fellow paid little further attention to my discourse except to dispute my observation that director and scenographer did not always find it easy to agree on a mutually-ideal lighting balance. He advised me that there is an establishment to the north of London where total harmony always prevails and the path of the lighting designer is forever smooth. Why should (indeed, how could) it ever be otherwise? Why indeed! How indeed!

...and lighting real

A few days later, I was enjoying a dress rehearsal as guest of a leading European opera house. The distinguished director and scenographer were English and frequently worked together. They were known to me but I was unknown to them. So I played fly-on-the-wall to their foot-stamping disagreements about whether the lighting balance should favour the actors or the set. Both of them displayed a rather alarming ignorance of the more basic facts of stage lighting. Perhaps if their talents had been tempered by just a touch more rationality, their vision might possibly have been communicated more positively to the audience. Fortunately, the resident lighting designer deployed the necessary cool logic and tact. His compromise saved the day.

2
Learning
To Use
Light

With no lighting schools outside the United States, my generation of European lighting designers had no alternative but to go to Yale or learn on the job, so we learned on the job. Since we were the first generation, there was no one to be apprenticed to. So we had to think on our feet, responding instantly to what we saw and heard. There were a few books on lighting, particularly those by Stanley McCandless, Harold Ridge, Fred Bentham, Percy Corry and Gillespie Williams, which we read avidly. We devoured Strand's catalogues and their magazine *Tabs*. The literature tended to describe where lighting had been and where it was now, rather than where it should be going, but all the writers shared our passion and there were some pointers to the future, mostly based on wishful thinking about how technology might develop. We were all inspired by Adolphe Appia's dream of space defined by light.

Our basic learning equipment was our eyes and ears. Each production weekend was a time for living dangerously; taking artistic risks was our only way to discover how light behaved and how it could be made to do what we wanted. We did this by the elegantly-simple method of relating cause to effect. We discussed light with anyone who would debate. We listened avidly to established producers, directors, designers, painters, stage managers and electricians – all those who had previously 'done the lighting' as part of their job. We listened because we realised that moving forward is speeded up by looking back into the vast reservoir of experience. But we subjected everything connected with lighting's past and present to critical analysis. Mistakes were inevitable and some of the rejected past has subsequently been restored. But quite a lot of lighting tradition was obstructing progress – it had to go and it did.

Our attempts to enter into dialogue with manufacturers were a little tricky at first because lighting designers were seen as something of an unnecessary intrusion into the established and cosy relationships enjoyed by manufacturers with theatre owners and producers. But we persisted and we won them over with the aid of hastily-acquired interpersonal skills which were being honed by our efforts to get working practices adapted to meet the rigours of lighting's new technologies and aspirations. We flew by the seat of our pants and it was an exciting time.

Lighting design has now progressed well beyond the point where basic skills can be acquired whilst busking under the pressures of a production weekend. Consequently, learning to light is becoming a more formalised process. Is this right? It certainly would seem much easier to grow up with something than be plunged into the end product. But should we really saddle fresh young minds with the results of our own erratic thinking? Would it, perhaps, be better to drop them in with a clear unprogrammed mind to bring fresh thinking to the problems? Alas, the stakes are just too high. Lighting is the last phase in the staging process and normally is not completed until just before the technical and dress rehearsals commence. It has to be nearly right first time; there may be *brief* opportunities for polishing but not for major reconstruction. Moreover, the pressures of time, and therefore money, have now increased to the point where unscheduled overtime due to inexpert management – or even hesitation – during the focusing and plotting can have severe budgetary consequences for the production's viability.

A sure sign that any new profession has established itself is the appearance of specialist educational programmes. While this is certainly to be welcomed, the process of moving towards more formal education methods poses sufficient problems to set the worry beads a-jangling. Formal education produces formal qualifications, and formal qualifications depend on formal examinations. It is easiest for examinations to assess skills that are measurable. These measurable skills, being largely factual, are easier to teach than the more intangible creative-thinking process which is the heart of any art. Thus the cornerstone of formal education – the syllabus – can become an exercise in teaching the possible rather than the desirable. It is simpler to construct a syllabus from subjects which can be easily taught and examined – the objective craft rather than the subjective art.

Craft examinations present no problem; indeed, qualification by examination is a necessary component of safety. What is to be resisted is that the art, because it is difficult to examine, should be accorded reduced status in the syllabus. No one sets out to do this consciously, but it is an easy situation to reach by default – particularly when coping with the resource problems involved in teaching such a subject in an educational climate where funding is geared to minimising the unit-cost per student.

Anyone studying for a degree in lighting design would do well to remember that tertiary education is not about being taught. The role of universities and colleges, particularly in the arts, is not so much teaching but providing an environment which is structured for learning. To some extent this includes the staff providing challenges for their students, but more fundamental is the opportunity for students to challenge themselves.

Today's lighting students have the benefit of information presented to them in a logical sequence, and they are placed in a series of projects which are designed to lead them through a structured exploration of all phases of the lighting process. However, learning still needs to be a process of active enquiry rather than passive assimilation. No information should be received as gospel. There are questions to be asked, superficial answers detected, and the real truth teased-out. There are established philosophies and procedures to be analysed. Perhaps for acceptance now, but possible reaction against later. Effects to be related to their causes. And, above all, the eye to be developed. Perhaps the lighting designer's major pieces of equipment are the eye and the eraser.

It is still possible to have a theatre career without going to theatre school. It is important that this opportunity remains, even if only for a decreasing few. The creation of a successful stage performance is something of a mysterious process which can accommodate some mavericks and anarchists. Any sensitive inquisitive person pitchforked into a theatre educates themselves by watching and asking. They can acquire an understanding of the nitty-gritty of lighting, albeit slowly and unsystematically. But there is a risk that the aesthetic purpose can remain a mystery enshrined in a huddle of figures at the production desk. Any theatre-education system must, however, be sufficiently flexible to accommodate opportunities for mid-life career development, including entry to, and exit from, stage lighting.

In a formal school-programme, the young lighting designer acquires a systematic understanding of the craft, and begins to explore the potential of the art. The structure of the programme will mirror professional practice, but introduce topics gradually so that the student is not overwhelmed with too much information or too many options at once. The stage lighting process has two interrelated phases: the development of visual ideas, and the realisation of these ideas for performance. Any lighting-education programme must concern itself with both these aspects simultaneously because the aesthetics and the practicalities are complementary: neither has any value on its own.

It is an oversimplification to consider the lighting designer as someone who has a complete vision of how the lighting of a particular production will look, and then converts that concept into reality. The visual ideas and their practical realisation feed off each other. The art and the science are integrated: one informs the other. While there is considerable theoretical virtue in allowing the imagination to roam freely, that imagination can be stimulated by an awareness of the technological possibilities. Moreover, the limitations of technology can stimulate by providing some welcome fences and signposts.

It can be very comforting for that blank sheet of paper to have some initial marks on it, even if they are negative indicators. Nevertheless, the starting point for any study of lighting must surely be a consideration of what we might aim to achieve in an ideal theatre in an ideal world. Initially, this will place no particular emphasis on lighting or on any other single aspect of the theatre experience. In parallel with an overview of dramatic performance in a wide range of contexts, both current and historical, students will be exposed to the practical processes of rehearsal and performance. This introductory study will embrace every form of live theatre – drama, opera, street, rock, dance, popular, puppet, musical, mime, cabaret, esoteric, etc. (the words have been listed in the order they came out of the hat). The objectives will be to provide the student with a broad understanding of the nature of theatre, its workings and its language. This will offer an appropriate foundation for further specialist studies, while serving a diagnostic role in assisting the potential lighting designer to assess whether this is really the career direction they wish to pursue.

A crucial question is whether formal education should continue at this point, or whether it should be interrupted by a period of work in a theatre. The current structure of most educational systems, including their funding, tends to be based on continuing with full-time formal studies until qualifying at a level which offers lifetime employment. But there are indications that the education system is becoming more flexible in response to the way in which the accelerating pace of technological change is affecting work patterns in all aspects of life. My view is that it is certainly necessary for the potential lighting designer to interrupt formal studies at some point to gain practical stage experience, both general and specialised. Just when this should happen, and whether it should be in one or more blocks, is debatable. If possible, it should be fully-paid employment rather than secondments – although these secondments vary enormously, even the best ones tend to have a flavour of observation rather than involvement with responsibility. My hunch is that if someone is still hooked on lighting after a foundation course, they should proceed to some initial specialist studies, followed by practical, theatre-gained, work experience before making a commitment to an in-depth lighting study programme.

If an advanced lighting design course is to achieve a level comparative to that normally expected of graduates in other professions, the logistics imply very small student numbers using very expensive resources. Given the consequent high unit-cost of such a course, and the relatively large numbers of students hoping for a career in lighting design, it is inevitable that recruitment will be highly selective. Prospective students will need to show high levels of commitment, aptitude and talent combined with an intuitive approach to interpersonal relationships. I would venture to suggest that these qualities can only be satisfactorily demonstrated and assessed in the environment of a working theatre. Whether the choice of a theatre-based career is the correct one, should be addressed by *actually working* in a live-theatre environment where, in addition, experience gained will be invaluable when it comes to deciding upon an area in which to specialise. If that specialist area is lighting, individual interests and aptitudes may lead towards a preference for technology rather than design.

At the risk of sounding tritely obvious, it has to be emphasised that the core of lighting design studies is *designing* lighting. This may take the form of production lighting or laboratory projects. Both situations are important; exploratory work, with time to take risks and try alternatives, has to be balanced with the reality of the pressures and paranoia of a production with a performance deadline. Inevitably, there are limited opportunities to light full-stage productions for presentation to an audience. Nevertheless, this experience is an essential part of the learning process for advanced students who, as they near graduation, should be capable of lighting even the plushest of drama school showcases. If this is not the case, the course teaching team will doubtless wish to debate whether their graduates are really lighting designers or just people who know about lighting design. The difference is not at all subtle and is the prime reason why student numbers on advanced courses have to be kept very small indeed.

Most practical lighting experience will, however, be gained through laboratory-style projects which, although simulating real situations and procedures, are not full productions intended for performance. This allows each project to be structured in such a way that students are able to explore particular aspects of lighting. Such projects also provide everyone in the group with an opportunity to design in a wide range of styles and to experiment with alternative solutions to the practical problems of implementing their designs.

In addition to group projects, students also need access to a lighting laboratory for personal experiments. Ideally, this laboratory will have the proportions of a small studio theatre, with an overall lighting grid and a wide range of the standard instruments made by the leading manufacturers. These practical explorations will be fed by a wide range of supporting studies and, although a basic understanding of the fundamental technology of how light behaves will be included, the emphasis will be on developing visual awareness and critical aesthetic judgement.

Lighting design has close affiliations with science and is dependent upon engineering. Nevertheless, its practitioners are primarily *artists*. Success is particularly dependent upon determination coupled with a self-criticism bordering on humility. Inquiry, discovery and relating cause to effect are at the heart of the learning process. Each and every day I carry on enquiring, hoping to discover more, and continuing to relate cause with effect. Learning to use light is an on-going process which I expect to continue until my final blackout.

So what's new?

Browsing in New York's Drama Bookshop, I discovered a reprint of Louis Hartmann's 1930 *Theatre Lighting*. "You do realise that this is not an up-to-date text", they warned, as I waved my dollars excitedly. Not up-to-date? What about this:

> "The man with 'theatre sense' will get more actual results with crude apparatus than a highly trained technician, who lacks this gift, with elaborate paraphernalia."

or this:

> "In some instances so many units were used that the scenery was virtually burned up with light. Quantity not quality was the result. It was the same reasoning that because one spoonful of medicine is effective, the entire bottle, taken at once, must be more so."

or this:

> "To obtain good results the men must be trained. It is just as necessary to coach the men who work the mechanical effects as it is to rehearse the actors. It is far better to do things in a simple way and do them well than to attempt to do them spontaneously in an elaborate manner and make a bungling job of it."

or this:

> "Knowledge acquired by experience is a great asset if we use it to guide improvement and new development; but if we try to use it as a standard or formula it is apt to hold us back."

Hartmann was David Belasco's chief electrician from 1901. Is he the first ever specialist lighting designer? He must surely be, at least, one of the first.

3
Styling
The Light

Accent, atmosphere, blending, composition, concentration, dimension, distribution, emotion, fluidity, illumination, location, modelling, mood, motivation, orchestration, painting, perception, plasticity, progression, punctuation, sculpture, selectivity, texture, and toning. These are just some of the many words used to describe the role of stage lighting. Most of them mean something. Many of them mean the same thing. Away from a specific production, all of them mean nothing. Except, perhaps, illumination – the audience expect to see. But other functions are optional – the result of a conscious choice determined by the role that lighting will play in the production style.

Scripts and scores can be realised for performance in many alternative styles. The preparation for staging each new interpretation starts with a search for an appropriate style for acting, movement, costume, scenery and lighting. It is particularly satisfying when we all, as a team, approach it with open minds, considering lots of possibilities. Gradually we home-in on one particular style, we then get hooked and believe that this is the only way to do it. Shortly after opening night, our minds open up again, we look at the production objectively and think "Well that was one way of doing it, *but next time!*"

Alas, a few directors and set designers have something approaching a doctrinaire attitude to style, and perhaps it is a sign of the coming of age of lighting design that one or two of its practitioners have also developed a rather rigid approach. There is also some geographical polarisation.

Anglo-American lighting tends to favour the sonority of large orchestras of small, fixed, tinted instruments, while parts of eastern Europe have a fondness for choirs of massed beamlights. The repertoire houses of central Europe rely on extensive follow-spotting to cope with the movement uncertainties of actors playing a wide range of roles on successive evenings – or singers jetting-in with negligible time for rehearsal.

Simultaneous productions of the same play in different styles is a relatively new development. Until well into the twentieth century, production style evolved so slowly that it seemed static for long periods. The pace of change over any theatre-goer's lifetime was such that we can identify periods of consistent style with such wide historical labels as Shakespearean, Jacobean, Georgian, Regency, Victorian, Edwardian etc., when anyone visiting a theatre knew with considerable certainty how the performance would be staged. Lighting was a strong influence on the evolution of these various period styles. Increased levels of illumination made possible by the invention of the Argand oil lamp enabled the actor to retreat from the thrusting forestage to behind the proscenium arch and a more integrated relationship with the scenery. This process was accelerated by gas light which also allowed more sophisticated fades and changes of colour. Limelight offered highly-intense directional beams and greater control over selective emphasis of particular areas of the stage. Electricity opened up vast new possibilities and now digital processing is a revolutionary tool with fresh capabilities continually emerging.

It is possible, therefore, to identify a series of historical production styles each of which has a lighting component. However, we very rarely try to replicate these historical styles on today's stage. Audiences make an essential contribution to a performance, and their perception is now conditioned by a very different lifestyle. But historical styles may well provide elements of an approach or just a springboard from which quite radically different ideas may evolve.

The early years of the twentieth century produced some lighting styles which became very fashionable for relatively brief periods. There was the limitless space of the cyclorama which liberated the theatre from the nearness of a wrinkled sky of painted canvas. That cyclorama, in turn, became a surface on which to play out some complex theories of the psychology of colour. A production of Twelfth Night, described in Harold Ridge's 1930 *Stage Lighting*, records a style based on colour washes:

Scene	Spirit of Scene	Lighting
Duke's palace	Love	Front – pink Back – blue
Olivia's room	Melancholy	Front – amber Back – green
Olivia's room	Drunken revelry	Front – blue Back – magenta
Olivia's garden	Reconciliation	Front – pink Back – moonlight green

The use of strong filter contrasts for emotional underlining and actor sculpting produced strong reactions, particularly from Brecht whose pursuit of clarity led a move to abandon many of light's new possibilities and let it revert to a simple bright continuous illumination.

Production styles and their lighting components cannot be generalised, so it is an oversimplification to give them names. Style is not a garnish applied from conveniently labelled sauce bottles. Style is not added but grows from within. Style reveals itself in a mass of integrated details which, meaningless by themselves, unite together to give a clarity of approach. Style establishes itself through a consistency of approach.

So where does the lighting designer look for clues? Directors' remarks may, just may, provide a hint. Howard Bay has summarised a certain type of these delightfully, if a touch cynically, as "I see it all sort of underwater" and "A fragile dream in the mind's eye of Dierdre." Directors have stimulated me with such triggering phrases as "Perhaps varnished like an old oil painting", "Purple is so ecclesiastical" and "Gaslight certainly has traces of green, but some sunlight also includes just a tinge of it." But, basically, it is mostly a matter of absorbing scripts, absorbing music, absorbing discussions and absorbing rehearsals. Being a sponge, albeit a critically-aware sponge. It is when mulling over ideas that lighting designers reach many of their real decisions – i.e. when they appear to be gazing vacantly into space.

Defining priorities can sharpen the mind: simplicity is often the road to clarity. Tentative suggestions can help to tease out a consensus of ideas from colleagues in the production team. The key question for the lighting designer is 'How will we use light in this production?' As a blunt question, asked at a production meeting, this can be a real conversation-stopper! But lighting decisions have to be made – corporate decisions by the production team. Everybody: director, choreographer, set and costume designers, lighting designer and author (if it is a new play) will all have their own lighting priorities. And so will the production manager handling the budget and schedules.

The answer to 'How will we use light in this production?' has to be teased out. Asking leading questions, suggesting different possibilities, establishing a consensus and integrating the lighting within the ideas of a team who hold corporate responsibility for the production under the leadership of the director. The search for style is not one based on logical decisions – particularly not a logic that can be explained in words, although there may be a purely visual logic in a sequence of images. Such an image sequence is right because it looks right, although it defies justification in words. I do not look at a stage for something that can be explained logically in words. I hope to see lighting pictures that make visual sense and help the totality of the performance. Light that integrates with the acting, the music, the scene, the costume, the movement, the words, the idea behind the words. All part of a search for a total theatre.

Lighting, like any other design process, is based upon a sequence of logical management decisions which provide a framework for creative imagination to flourish. Creative decisions have to be made in a logical sequence, even if the actual decisions are illogical. A short and snappy definition of art might be 'creative illogical decisions'. This could lead to a definition of design as 'creative illogical decisions taken in a logical sequence'. Logic also provides a useful fall-back. If you run out of exciting illogical ideas, you can always fall back on a few well-tried logical ones. And you may sometimes have to disguise hunches as logic in order to sell a crazily illogical idea to the rest of the production team.

Lighting designers do not impose their ideas. They are members of a creative and management team. Lighting designers share, in common with every member of the team, a corporate responsibility for the visual environment on the stage – a visual environment which supports the performers in interpreting the text and musical score. Stylistic matters agreed by the team for lighting, as for everything else, will be in terms of broad policy. The lighting designer, like all the other specialists, then attends to the detailed work within the agreed broadly-based framework.

Creative thinking may seem a rather pompous phrase for coming up with an idea but it is a better term than another piece of current jargon – 'innovative creative response' – which is just new market-speak for what used to be called a *gimmick*. Gimmickry is not what real theatre is about. The best creative decisions just *happen* – an idea appears from somewhere; for me, it is often little more than a simple gut feeling, although it might be more poetic to ascribe its origins to the soul. Presumably, it derives from some deeply-subconscious interaction between all sorts of assorted, miscellaneous bits of information and experiences filed away in the recesses of the brain.

When an idea appears, the critical decision area is recognising whether that idea is any good or not. This, I suppose, is what is known as aesthetic judgement, another faculty that seems to reside in the gut – or soul! The search for style varies with the performance medium and to a large extent arises out of it. Speech, song and movement, whether in the pure forms of drama, opera and dance, or in their endlessly possible mixtures, will influence the overall style.

All aspects of a drama production stem from the text. I, personally, do not find script-reading an easy process. To some people, the text leaps off the page – they hear voices and visualise the characters. Not me, I find it very hard work. I always start off earnestly but usually find myself less-than-totally gripped. My eye starts to skim, hoping to find any stage directions. So I start again and try to concentrate. But often, when I hear the cast read through the play, I am amazed how it comes to life. In all honesty, I must confess to finding myself often thinking "Well, this doesn't seem such a lousy play after all."

My text analysis should provide me with a breakdown of the *mechanics* of the play. I persevere until it does. But, to find out what the play is really about, I have to rely, to a large extent, on vibrations from the rest of the production team. This is not such a problem today as it was in my youth. At that time, texts were usually performed at their face value with audiences allowed to develop, consciously or subconsciously, their own interpretation of any subtext. However, many of today's directors are deconstructers who are convinced that authors do not realise the hidden ideas that motivate their writing. In such situations, all of us, actors and audience included, are totally dependent upon the director's interpretation of the text.

Musicals are much easier to analyse than plays. They readily break down into the sequence that we call a running order (any problem seems to get easier if broken down into sequences of smaller and smaller problems). The music says a lot about the light, and this also has become easier during my lifetime because more shows are now recorded. In my youth I lit lots of operas that hadn't been staged or heard since their first per-formances in a previous century. My score-reading is pretty lousy and my family will never escape from the memory of my attempts to play all the soloists, chorus and orchestra on a flute of which my technical mastery was only notional and brought a whole new meaning to the expression "Once more, with feeling." Nowadays, rare operas tend to be recorded *before* they are performed, so you can play them while you work. Musicals are invariably recorded immediately after the opening performance, and even new unperformed musicals usually have some kind of demo-tape made to help convince the money-people to back the show.

I find that I get more feeling for light from music than from words. One of my most positive experiences was working with the great German director Carl Ebert. He had been an actor and I seem to find it easier to work with directors who have acted or danced. They seem to communicate better and they also seem to understand the agony of searching for something when you don't quite know what you're looking for. I can still feel Ebert's hand squeeze my arm during rehearsal as he said "Francis, my dear, can you hear the light?" After a run-through, I could almost tell the number of major light cues we would need by counting the bruises.

How useful is research to the lighting designer? Digging out the background to the text, studying the historical period, reading the novel if it is an adaptation, looking at old movie versions, looking up pictures and reviews of previous productions, reading commentaries on the play or its author if it is a classic. All this can be dangerous. I tend to belong to the school of thought which says go back to the basic text and\or music score and, initially at least, only work from there. Just try to get to the core of the author's original and do not get confused by the approach of other productions or by the response of critics. So, I have rarely found this kind of literary research valuable. I never read the 'novel of the play' before, although I nearly always find it an enjoyable read *after* the show has opened.

Picture research is valuable to any designer – not words but visual images. Pictures are a key resource for set and costume designers, but images offer a lot of help for the lighting designer too – particularly images which contain light that has been processed by another artist's eye. The light in photographs can be helpful but, often, the use of light in paintings provides the most fruitful research material. Much of my own most fundamental research has been carried out as I walk along the road; observing how light falls on buildings and people.

The lighting designer's search for visual images tends to come, possibly during but certainly after, that key point in the design process when we are striving to establish the production style. Looking at a designer's model may trigger a search for the way that certain photographers or painters, or painters of a particular period, used light. It may be a half-remembered picture we want to look at again, or just a hunt for something that will help. This usually means flicking through books, but soon it could mean searching for pictures by accessing a visual image bank via our personal computer screens. The really difficult part of the search for style is communication. In all my years as a lighting designer I have never felt inhibited by my lack of any detailed knowledge of electric or electronic theory. And, as for photometrics, well I would not recognise a foot-candle if I met one walking down the road. Indeed, I have only recently discovered that 'Lux' is something more than a washing powder! No, I do not feel a need to know more about these things, but I do wish I could draw. Not technical drawing: I am not very good at that either, but it doesn't seem to matter as the crew seem to be able to read my plans.

By drawing I mean *sketching*. I would love to be able to sketch alternatives while we talk. "Do you mean like this…, or like that?" My ideal director would pick up a pencil and say "Well, I rather see it like this." Although scene designers have the ability, surprisingly few draw light. Life is always easier if the designer draws a storyboard: it helps to encourage the director to use the set in the way that its designer intended. It helps even more if this storyboard includes some indication of the way the designer imagines the scene will be lit. Drawing light is not easy but it is often helps to start off with black paper because nothing is seen until there is light.

Perhaps drawing with pencils is not the answer in these hi-tech times. Soon, we will no longer sit around a model talking about light, trying to find meaningful words, shining anglepoise lamps and flashlights from various angles through bits of filter. We'll be sitting around a video screen – on the screen will be a realistic depiction of what can be realised, in practice, on the stage. "Is this how we see the light?" the lighting designer will say, whilst simultaneously providing an on-screen demonstration of his or her suggested approach to the lighting. Then, it will not be my pencil but my mouse that the director and set designer will grab. We may not all want to work that way, but the possibility is going to be here – and soon. Meanwhile, I work to the established rule of thumb, bashing away with the old inadequate words. What are our expectations of the range of contributions that light may make to a stage production? The basics don't change, although current fashion tends to be an overriding factor – sometimes overriding common sense. Fashion, however, tends to be mostly just a shift of emphasis.

Whatever the style of light, there is almost certainly a need for the actors to be visible. Moments when an actor is not fully-visible can be very dramatic, but they have to be very controlled and cannot last too long. The actor's face and the dancer's limbs need to be seen if their characterisation is to project to the audience. If we have less-than-ideal visibility, it should be a matter of choice rather than neglect. There is also a virtually universal need to support the visual stage environment by enhancing the third dimension to make the stage pictures as sculptural as possible. Any flatness should occur only as a matter of choice not neglect. But beyond that we have many options.

Shall we use light to focus the attention of the audience on selected areas of the stage? Shall we use light to create atmosphere? How natural will the light be? Will it make logic in terms of suns, moons, stars and chandeliers? Or will it be abstract? Or somewhere in between? Light is the most important means by which to control the fourth dimension of a stage environment – *time*. How will we use this possibility of dynamic changes? Perhaps consciously, perhaps subconsciously, perhaps both, perhaps neither? And so on. Once we have a team idea of the lighting style (or think we have – we can never be sure until well into the first lighting rehearsal on stage), we can move on to analysing the structure of the production. Establishing where light is required, and where it is not required, its quality, its colour, its quantity.

We need to spend a lot of time in the rehearsal room. We rarely do. Not because we do not want to, but because we cannot afford to. Time spent in the rehearsal room has three major benefits. The obvious one is observing the mechanics of the production, particularly scene locations and actor moves. This is most valuable in the later phases of rehearsal. Possibly more important, particularly in the earlier phases, is getting the *feel* of the production. Watching and absorbing can trigger visual ideas. Just being present in the rehearsal room builds confidence in the actors that the lighting is not just going to be some monstrous technology, imposed on their performances and perhaps even threatening them.

The key to finding a lighting style that is sympathetic to all other aspects of the production lies in balancing the contrasts and pacing the timing. Lighting is ultimately about a balanced contrast within each picture and a balanced contrast from picture-to-picture. It is about pace – accelerations and decelerations. Lighting has to be paced towards orgasm; going at it with a frenzy is a recipe for anticlimax. There are two great potholes on the road to lighting design: too much too soon, and too little too late. Like all members of the creative team who support the performers' efforts to communicate the work of writer and composer to an audience, lighting designers must constantly remember the dance of the seven veils:

- Do not drop them all at once
- Reveal gently
- Peel
- Tantalise.

The last one to fall is often a disappointing anticlimax. But this can be disguised by good timing. The final arbiter of aesthetic judgement has to be the eye of the lighting designer, subject to that designer being sympathetic to the response of the rest of the team, and a firm understanding that the last word must remain with the director who, as team leader, carries ultimate responsibility for the entire production.

Illusions of reality

I met a sad scene-designer who wanted her play to look soft and hazy when it remained stubbornly harsh and clear. She wondered what was wrong with the lighting. I ventured to suggest that the lighting was splendid (it was not my design) but only *distance* could add a soft, hazy enchantment to an audience view. "Thrust it not harshly into the laps of the audience but let it be set softly upstage and (with voice fading to a whisper as my self-confidence ebbed) framed by a false proscenium." She kept her cool, for her hang-ups are rationalised to the point where they barely hang. Patiently she explained the delicate nature of the actor–audience relationship. "Rhubarb," I cried, for I was schooled in rough theatre and my hang ups are not at all well hung, "theoretical rhubarb."

We then partook of a couple of friendly jars and agreed to divide the acting profession into two basic categories. No, not those that can find their light and those that cannot, but those who can project themselves through ten gauzes from sixty feet upstage and those who cannot project themselves when they are thrust into the laps of their audience.

Pausing to admire the last seconds of a sunset which she dismissed as celestial lighting designer's kitsch, we went our separate ways into the night. Her moon was probably white, mine was distinctly blue. I do not know her thoughts, although I am sure she had some for it is logic rather than divinity that shapes her end. In matters theatrical, I am neither logical nor divine: my responses are merely sensuous. But that night I pondered and offer my thoughts in that unanswerable form, the rhetorical question.

Not so long ago when we looked at a stage picture from the audience and then inspected the backstage mechanics, we were amazed at the illusion, the deception, the economy of painted mountain, of canvas wall, of hessian silk. Today that trip through the pass-door frequently reveals not magic but a massively engineered structure of real material, which often looks considerably less than real from the front. Why *has so much from so little become so little from so much*? Is this an example of the art that conceals art?

The visual elaboration of Restoration Masque and Victorian Shakespeare blurred communication between playwright and audience. In both cases a reaction produced simpler staging. Advocates of minimal stage settings, constructed from real materials, are vociferous in their claims of playwright supremacy: but do they in fact perhaps deny the interpreting actor a supportive scenic environment? Their advocacy is persuasive and logical but does this rationality sometimes tend to obscure the instinctive responses of the senses? How often is the search for truth an intellectual rationalisation of the hunt for gimmickry? Do we tend towards a theatre for 'Theatreman and his analysts' when we need a theatre for 'Everyman and his children'? Should theatre embrace its natural illusion (for in computer jargon, illusion is surely theatre's default mode) or pursue reality? If anti-illusion is artistically desirable – and I have indicated my personal doubt – it bears little inspection under the microscope of cost effectiveness: may there perhaps be a degree of truth in that old managerial chestnut "Shall I see it from the Box Office?" And then I realised that my ponderings were close to the theoretical rhubarb that I had been so vocal in condemning. So I ceased my ponders, said good night to the blue moon and faxed the sad designer thus "You cannot use light to make a thrust production look soft and hazy, but you *can* use light to make a proscenium production look either soft and hazy, *or* harsh and clear."

4
Effective
Effects

I was once credited in a programme with 'Lightning by' and I laughed. But I screamed when my credit announced 'Lighting Effects by'. This is a world away from the critical tribute of 'Effective lighting by'! Effects are defined in my Little Oxford dictionary as 'sounds and visual features as accompaniment to a play'. The Concises, both Collins and Oxford, mention light, include film and television, but stay firmly with *accompany*. This implies something running in parallel rather than integrated with the action, distracting rather than supporting. Bernard Shaw's response to Basil Dean's 1923 demonstration of the possibilities of the newly-fashionable cyclorama was doubtless slightly tongue-in-cheek but nevertheless had a fundamental truth: "I'll take good care ye'll not use any of those contraptions in my plays, young man. The audience would be so busy staring at your clouds they wouldn't listen to my words."

The only justification in using effects as graffiti might possibly be as a result of despairing at the quality of the performers or the work they are performing. Stage lighting is used to conceal and to reveal. Used crudely, however, it can expose. Attempts to use lighting to distract may succeed momentarily but, like most such efforts to enliven a weak performance, they often succeed in emphasising its creative poverty. Effects used as an integral part of a production can be very supportive. This often means deploying them subtly so that they underline points which are being made in dialogue, music and movement. However, subtlety does not mean underplaying them. Everything on a stage needs to be a positive statement: the key to subtlety of effect is precise timing and this means a clean start and no milking.

Repetition quickly becomes boring and, in the case of some optical effects, prolonged exposure reduces the effect's credibility and may even play tricks with the eye. Snow is a prime example of this: they eye gets confused and the snow can appear to stop momentarily. All optical effects have to be used with care because they are projecting two-dimensional images of three-dimensional objects. Achieving convincing depth requires superimposing the light from several projectors with different focuses. My most successful snow storm used over a dozen projectors, four on to a front gauze and the remainder on to the various structures of the scene behind. It was the opening to the third act of *La Boheme* and lasted a bare thirty seconds before slowly fading out. However, despite the mess on the floor, I usually prefer to use fluttering paper or polystyrene flakes caught in a crosslight.

The answer to the two-dimensional projection dilemma is often to abandon pictorial images and aim for the quality of the *reflected* light that is produced. Shimmering light of the appropriate colour is usually more convincing than pictures of fire and water. But only a full integration can lead to the audience suspending their disbelief. Some years ago I designed the lighting for a play which required a church vicarage to be consumed by flames on the intimate stage of London's *Criterion*. Projected pictorial flames, in varying softness of focus, were mixed with shimmering reflected firelight while red and amber floods were flickered on their dimmers. Smoke was injected until it became one of the projection surfaces. The crackle of the fire and the crashing of timbers grew stereophonically. We were nearly there but something was missing. It was supplied by two firemen who unrolled a flat hose along the front of the stage. As this hose gradually filled with water (actually, it was compressed air) even I began to believe in the fire – especially as the timely arrival of the water appeared to be the cause of the fire beginning to die down just before the fade to blackout and interval curtain.

Once we are in the realm of shimmering impressions rather than quasi-naturalistic pictures, equipment becomes smaller and cheaper. Optical projectors with motor-driven glass discs can be replaced by standard profile-spots with stationary gobos given an illusion of movement by simple perforated rotating discs in the front colour frame runners. Success is dependent on focus and speed adjustment of the superimposed gobo images from several sources. During my working life, affordable remote speed-variation is probably the most important development in effects projection I've seen. I can remember crawling along the stage floor, behind a groundrow, to start an effect-disc because the cue was too late in the scene for the spring capacity of the clockwork motor. I have wasted a substantial part of my working life in fighting with the rubber tyres on potters-wheel speed adjusters!

Projected images have a translucent quality and we need to ensure that this is compatible with the materials used in construction of the scenic environment. Indeed, differing image quality is a major concern of any lighting designer working in a mixed-media situation. Film, video and slide provide images with a capability for flexibility of manipulation far beyond traditional scenic materials, particularly in respect of changes of location or scale. However, when these images are totally realistic, they rarely feel visually comfortable. The departure from literal reality needs to be accompanied by projection on to surfaces which do not proclaim themselves to be screens. And whether the slides are generated by paint, photography or computer graphics, an emphasis of the depth dimension by exaggeration of the light and shade in the artwork will increase the credibility of the stage environment. Totally realistic projection does have its place, but that place tends to be in the realm of contributing a documentary commentary on the action rather than an integral part of the environment. There are, of course, exceptions. We are talking here of using two-dimensional media in support of a traditional live stage performance. There are occasions, such as Prague's *Laterna Magica*, where the slides and film provide the heart of the show and the actors are the auxiliaries.

The same situation could be said to apply to megastar rock tours where the performance has to match audience expectation of participating in an event of evangelistic scale. For most of the audience in a big stadium, the band are distant dots and the relevance of their music is the recordings which helped create a legend in which the audience wish to share by proximity. For a realisation of anticipation, the prime need is an assault on the senses by every possible aural and visual effect that can contribute to creating and maintaining a rising tension. There is an insatiable demand for ever more complex flash-and-chase sequences combined with the gyrations of motorised lights with instant changes of colour, gobo and focus. But unless they are deployed with great care, such effects can defeat their own aim. Flashing, chasing and gyrating become so normal that we barely notice them. Stillness, by contrast, can be the more dramatically-arresting event. In the pop music industry, dynamic movement of light has gone beyond mere fashion. It has become a doctrine.

However, rock's relentless pursuit of light movement, supported with resources to fund research and development, has had generous spin-offs for more traditional forms of staging. The laser-generated image is not only three-dimensional but can flutter in space with help from nothing more substantial than a little smoke. I know of nothing better to accompany the rubbing of Aladdin's lamp, providing magic and momentarily distracting the audience from the mechanics of the cave transformation. But it is the small, almost subliminal, subtle effects that make the most effective contri-bution. Fibre-optic stars on a black cloth provide a totally convincing night sky and their delicate flicker can disturb the eye just enough to make wires disappear so that flying fairies really float.

As for that 'Lightning by' credit... well, we almost have the technology. We no longer have the problems of insufficient brightness followed by long decay-time, although we could use a faster recharge-time on flash units. So we can concentrate on ensuring that our forked lightning does not strike in the same place twice and that our sheet lighting does not expose the mechanics of the stage masking.

Dangerous signals

I have learned not to count on the old saying that "It'll be all right on the night." And warning bells ring when I hear...

'They' say	But *really* mean...
"Let's do it all with light!"	*We have run out of ideas.*
"Money is a bit tight, could we project the scenery?"	*Only ever asked by people with no experience of projection.*
"My agent's cousin saw last night's preview."	*And knows exactly what we need to change.*
"The director just does not seem to know how to use my set."	*I am a frustrated director.*
"The set isn't quite what I expected."	*Why not, it's an exact ×25 blow-up of the model.*

   ...and, in my experience, despite what 'they' say, a bad rehearsal rarely means a good performance.

5
Lighting With
Optimum
Resources

Is lighting really as important as all we lighting-people would like to think it is? I have to confess to a nagging worry that many theatre-people, myself included, become so blinkered by our own specialism that we lose sight of how it fits into the whole. This is understandable. Indeed it is so under-standable that it is almost inevitable. A life in theatre is not a rational career choice for anyone other than a committed idealist. The process of staging productions is so intense that it induces a single-minded concentration on reaching out towards perfection in each and every area. This allows little scope for seeking a balance between the relative effectiveness of different contributions to the production mix.

The reality of budgets, schedules and human frailty makes some degree of compromise inevitable. But the need for this compromise is rarely acknowledged. Compromise tends to be reached by default rather than by considered debate. This can lead to the 'total' being rather less than the potential offered by sum of its parts. Striving for an ideal in our own special contribution, while taking a balanced overview of how the scale of that contribution integrates with everyone else's, requires a very delicate degree of pragmatism. The proportions of production time and money devoted to lighting have been causing me concern for some forty years. As a young stage manager, I became involved in lighting, not so much because of a passion to create, but a desire to get the action moving so that we could all get to bed before sunrise. I am just as concerned today because I worry that theatre may possibly stand poised on the brink of being a victim of the dinosaur syndrome.

The theatre-world claims that its major growth area has been in quality. Few would deny exciting surges, particularly in the sixties and early seventies. But subsequent years seem to have been rather more notable for expansion in technology and bureaucracy. Growth follows a natural progression from minimum to maximum, and somewhere in between lies an optimum where there is a flattening of the curve of improvement plotted against expenditure of time and money. The search for optimum has never been attractive to people in creative fields like arts and politics; minima and (particularly) maxima are much more exciting than the optimum. I get a growing feeling that we may have become so fixated on going for the maximum, that theatre may be on the way to becoming so bloated that it may be unable to feed itself.

This is not a new concern. Most eras of theatre, from the Roman Arena through the Jacobean Masque, Victorian Melodrama and Contemporary Musical, have demonstrated a compulsive desire to expand. In 1794, playwright Richard Cumberland declared of the new Drury Lane: "Henceforward theatres for spectators rather than playhouses for hearers ...the splendours of the scenes, the ingenuity of the machinist and the rich display of dresses, aided by the captivating charms of music now in a great degree supersede the labours of the poet." Such growth tends to invoke reaction and a return to the basics of planks and a passion. But success triggers a growth which has a habit of moving relentlessly towards establishing new thresholds of 'maximum', bypassing any apparent attempt at determining the optimum.

The size of lighting rigs and the knob-count on control desks has climbed resolutely upwards, while the labour-saving potential of each new hardware development has been absorbed by growth in the numbers used. The best of our lighting design is as good as it ever was (no, not better, although the 'go for maximum' syndrome needs the comfort of assuming that it is better). But how about the middle-of-the-road stuff? It is certainly brighter, but are eyes and teeth always getting a sufficiency of the visibility which is at the core of any actor-support system? This brings us back to balance: the more one works with light, the more one discovers how to increase the effect of one light by fading another light down or out. Audiences are protected from escalating brightness by the irises in their eyes, so excessive increases in light intensity become counter-productive. But what about *sound*, now increasing in volume to the point where musical intervals are becoming compressed to vanishing point? So far, the only people to have succeeded in developing irises in their ears seem to be some sound operators.

The desire to maximise is understandable. I am no stranger to the compelling wish to ensure the success of my contribution to a production by hanging lights for every contingency, then adding a belt to the braces. And I certainly tend to follow this through to the limitations imposed by my slice of the budget. But I have discovered time and time again that elimination of equipment, by extended agonising during the planning phase, tends to result in lighting that is not only cheaper, but cleaner and crisper.

In the days of four-poster bedrooms, fundamental advice was often embroidered on samplers and hung where it could offer the last word at night and the first in the morning. For a lighting designer, the most apt motto would probably be "A lighting designer's best friend is an eraser" a phrase I have been known to doodle on my drawing board. In tomorrow's world it would, perhaps, be more appropriate to have a little box especially programmed to pop-up on the computer's screen and declare "A lighting designer's best friend is the Delete key."

The eraser often has to be set to work in conjunction with a pocket calculator. The first draft of a lighting plan frequently exceeds the rental budget for additional equipment. Every light erased allows a minus entry on the calculator, and the wise designer will keep rubbing out until the figure is at least ten per cent under budget to allow a margin for the inevitable contingencies. The first draft is also likely to require more than the designated schedule times, particularly the length of the slot allocated for focusing. Time is much more difficult to calculate than money because there are so many interacting factors. How accessible are the lights? How well maintained are they? How experienced are the crew?

What is the ratio of simple parcans and focus-spots with their three adjustments, to complex profile-spots which can have up to eleven? It is a calculation which has no place for optimism.

It is difficult to overestimate the knock-on effect that a big rig may have on the viability of a production. Actual equipment rental costs are only the beginning. Production labour-costs may be inflated not so much by the numbers of lighting crew, but by the other technicians who have to be paid for long waiting periods during extended lighting calls. Extended technical preparation time can mean curtailing dress rehearsals with the actors or delaying the first night. Once open, a big rig need not require more per-formance running crew, but is likely to involve more maintenance. None of this is significant under the mega-investment conditions of a blockbuster musical intended for the international market, but it could mean life or death for anything less grandly financed.

Budgets and schedules provide reactive reasons for seeking to retreat from heavy lighting rigs. A more proactive response would be the use of a smaller rig because it might serve the production better. In my own expe-rience – not just as designer, but as a member of many audiences – light from a smaller number of sources is more likely to have a cleaner crisper look. Even when the rig seems big, the number of instruments alive in each lighting state may be relatively small. My eyes have taught me that a lot of instruments alight at low intensities is a sure recipe for a muddy look.

While optimum may be closer to minimum than to maximum, it is by no means synonymous with minimum. There is, for example, a limit to the extent in which several narrow-angle spotlights can be replaced by a smaller number of wide-angle types. When an area of stage is lit by one wide cone from a single instrument, actors at each extremity of the area will be illuminated from significantly different angles. Furthermore, some lighting styles, which have become increasingly fashionable in the final decades of our century, evolved from the concept of using one single powerful instrument to emulate the sourcing of natural light. However, one such light relies on indirect reflections to light the shaded side of the actor's face. While this is the basis of lighting in nature, the reflected light may not be sufficiently controlled to provide the correct level for the actor to project in a large theatre. Scenery needs careful design of material, construction and textural finish if it is to reflect in a similar way to the natural surfaces which it represents. The reflected light may still require a little back-up from a few discreet instruments but, if used correctly, only the lighting designer should be consciously aware of their contribution.

A large rig can be difficult to balance and a small rig offers fewer possibilities. But, although rigs of the optimum size are easiest to handle in the theatre, they require much more planning work at the drawing board. The function of each instrument has to be scrutinised and justified. Priorities have to be rigorously assessed. It is hard work and it takes a long time but the resultant savings in budget and schedule, combined with a cleaner crisper look, can be very rewarding. And new technology, in the form of remotely-focusable lighting instruments with impeccable memories, would seem to offer most potential benefits to lighting designers who wish to approach the optimum.

Let's do it!

I know a rather disreputable fellow. His fundamental philosophy is that *if something is worth doing, then it is worth doing it badly.* This fellow believes that the quality of performance is not as important as the quality of the work performed.

He despairs of directors who will not trust the words or the music. He abhors deconstruction. He deplores the exponential growth of administrative procedures which seem to displace author, actor and audience as the primary purpose of theatre.

He believes that the function of the critical pen is not to so much to pronounce an assessment, but to inform on the nature of the work and record the essence of its performance. He worries that conventional criticism has made audiences feel obliged to sit in judgement and devise conversationally acceptable responses, distancing themselves from the performance by responding to it in a spirit of objective analysis rather than subjective submission.

He seeks a sensual theatre which strikes through to an immediate emotional response which leaves the senses with a stimulating aftertaste. He has discovered that the real impact of yesterday at the theatre does not hit him until the day after tomorrow.

He enjoys 'rough theatre'. It is fun. It has guts, gusto and a short rehearsal period. It is cheap and cheerful. It is noisy without microphones, elegant without chandeliers. It comes from the heart and it strikes at the soul. It defies logical analysis.

He loves 'rough lighting'. Not the roughness of a light that distracts with hard edges, misses actors' faces and makes their shadows walk tall across the sky. But a rough lighting that is broad slashes of colour, stark downlighters, and wham-bam-slam cross-cuts – all breathing with the words and the music.

He is rarely disappointed in a theatre. He always enters in a spirit of hope but he knows that the writing, the designing, the discussing, the rehearsing and the performing can only ignite into magic if an unidentifiable catalyst is present. He can trace little correlation between this magic and the conventional resources of buildings, materials and people. The vital spark seems to be a script or score which stimulates the executants into an enthusiasm which is transmitted to their audience.

And so this awful chap has come to believe that *if something is worth doing, then it is worth doing it badly.* Of course, he would rather do it magnificently well, but he is certain that it is much better to do it badly than not do it all. Who is he? Who is this despicable fellow?

It's Me.

6
Control
Boards

Discussion about boards tends to be obscured by differences between lighting *design* and lighting *operation*. For lighting design, most boards are equal, but for operation some boards may be considerably less equal than others. It was not always thus. Once upon a time it was necessary for lighting designers to consider the control consequences of each and every cue decision. They certainly had to understand the operational philosophy, and preferably the detailed operational procedures, of any system they encountered. Different dimmers had different characteristics, particularly in relation to speed of response, and in many cases these characteristics changed with the electrical load placed on the dimmer.

Some desks were only comfortable with rapid changes of groups of channels all moving by the same percentage, while others were more sympathetic to a few selected channels making slow moves with better accuracy. Few systems delivered a proportional fade: unless designer or operator intervened by dividing a cue into a sequence of part-cues, dimmers travelling shorter distances reached their new level before those travelling longer distances.

The time available to prepare a cue during performance was much more critical than the actual running time of the cue itself. Consequently, lighting designers constantly had to consider whether it would be possible to have a cue at all at a particular point. And if it were possible, how complex that cue could be.

In the mid-sixties, the dimmer problem was simplified, almost overnight, by the thyristor. All dimmers now have a similar response, and that response is independent of the load on the dimmer. By 1970, memory boards were feasible, by the mid-seventies they were established, and by the end of that decade they had become commonplace. There was virtually no limit to the number of possible cues that could be recorded for immediate, unlimited and accurate playback, with all channels moving proportionally unless the designer desired otherwise. Intensity control had become, and remains, no longer an issue. The designer is freed to concentrate upon the painting of pictures rather than on the mechanics of reproducing the paintings.

The actual plotting process has been enormously simplified by memory boards. We no longer need these agonisingly-long, detailed sessions where we checked every position by getting an assistant stage manager to walk the actors' moves. Now we can quickly rough-out the broad intention then complete the fine balancing throughout the sequence of technical and dress rehearsals. The basic requirements of light-control have been met, and lighting designers have reached the point where they should no longer feel constrained by device limitations – except, perhaps, by those imposed with the simplest non-memorising systems. However, there are still some topics which excite control buffs and enable manufacturers to launch a seemingly endless flow of newer models.

In traditional forms of theatre, designing and operating tend to be distinct roles. However, the shorter the run the more feasible it becomes for designers to operate – in the spirit of composers playing their own concerti. A designer–operator needs to be at the auditorium production desk for rehearsal, and in the control box for performance. So the entire desk has to be mobile or have its key operational functions duplicated in a portable designer's-unit. I adopted designer–operation at *Glyndebourne* in 1964 when the technology available required chunky multicore cabling and racks of electromagnetic relays. Many of today's desks can be tucked under the arm and require only a single slender screened-cable link to the dimmers. Alternatively, most of the operational functions can be duplicated in a small hand-held unit which resembles a sophisticated pocket calculator.

Using this technology, it is possible for an operator in the lighting box to run cues during rehearsals while the designer in the auditorium experiments with levels and re-records any desired amendments into the memories. Another format of portable designer-control provides access to channels for adjustment by touching a light-pen against graphic symbols on a 'magic sheet' formed by overlaying charts on to a digitiser. Alternatively, adjustments to the plot may be prepared on a laptop computer, away from the theatre if desired, and then fed into the board's memory.

I believe that direct designer hands-on 'light painting' with a magic-sheet type of palette will replace the traditional numbers dialogue between designer and operator. However, I am concerned that such procedures, by reducing operator involvement, might diminish their interest in the lighting and their understanding of what the designer is trying to achieve. Maintaining the quality of the lighting on a day-to-basis is dependent upon the operator not only identifying any lights with blown lamps or knocked focus, but having sufficient knowledge of the rig to be able to take compensating action if a light or an actor ends up in the wrong place.

By improving operator–designer communications during rehearsal – with the operator looking at the stage while adjusting levels as requested by the designer – the operator is better able to develop an understanding of the production and, hopefully, become committed to its success. Furthermore, operators are a very useful source of information on how the lighting looks from upstairs, and their involvement can be enhanced by a certain amount of thinking aloud by the designer.

For me, the really important piece of equipment that current new technology brings to the production desk is the simple video monitor showing the current intensity level of each channel. This has abolished the need for the endless designer question "What is channel 37 at?" Indeed, from the designer's point of view, the provision of a monitor on the production desk is a far more significant innovation than many of the much-trumpeted function knobs which proliferate on every new machine to hit the market. Similarly, the most welcome features of the latest hand-held control units are the facilities which enhance these controls for their primary use which is, in most theatres, as a *rigger's* control. For this particular lighting designer, the most important feature is *remainder dim* which fades out all channels except the one currently selected for focusing. While focusing, it is often necessary to recall several channels to check the overlap of individual beams. For safety and speed during focusing, any blackout – even momentarily – is undesirable. When using earlier rigger control-units without a remainder-dim key, the designer has to remember the numbers of all live channels in order that they can be individually dimmed. Another example of a rather simple facility being a designer priority.

Perhaps the most useful design facility to be added to control systems in recent years is *soft patching* which allows any channel number to be assigned to any dimmer. This is particularly advantageous for touring when each light on the rig can have the same number from week-to-week so that, if the systems are compatible, cue data can be fed in from disc. Even if the systems are incompatible, it is still easier to key-in manually if there is no need to keep referring to a number conversion chart.

When it comes to operation, two broadly alternative approaches emerged many years ago in pre-computer days. These may be conveniently labelled *organ loft* and *mission control*. The organists are primarily concerned with playability, whereas the missionaries recognise that the language of light is numerical – cue numbers, channel numbers, dimmer numbers, instrument numbers and filter numbers. Number-lovers have tended to be prominent in recent years, but there may have to be a swing towards more playability with desks increasingly required to integrate remote-movement functions with their traditional control of intensity. There are already some indications of this in the jargon. 'At the touch of a button' has had a long run as the standard cliché for expressing operational simplicity in an electronic age. 'Keystroking' seems to be the favoured replacement. Microchip technology is making control surfaces so sensitive that they will soon be able to respond to the difference between an admiring glance and a dirty look – and entire emotional gamut in between.

Meanwhile, 'stroking' is a computer word with welcome playability overtones: it implies that the timing is rather more under operator control than when a mere touching initiates the recall of a programmed action.

Whether as touchers of buttons, strokers of keys, wavers of light pens, clickers of mice, or merely carriers of luggage towards automatic doors, we are all beneficiaries of developments in control technology that have almost overtaken the wilder fantasies of sci-fi dreamers. Even the voice-activated dimmer is reported to be imminent. But is the loss of physical involvement to be regretted? Or will that not matter to generations who have never known the pleasure of pulling a dimmer-lever as if drawing a pint of ale, of wheeling a grandmaster with the swell of the orchestra, or even just experiencing the finely-detailed muscular pressures involved in handling miniaturised master-faders during a gauze dissolve?

However, the (current) major divide in control systems goes far deeper than playability, although in some respects is related to it. This is the transatlantic divide which set America and Europe on different paths from the very first memory systems. When Britain added computer processing to lighting control, most theatres were using multipreset boards, and so the new technology was used to memorise complete cue states in order to provide what was essentially an infinite number of presets. In America, the big impulse to memorise came later and, because it came from Broadway (*Chorus Line* – 1975), the jump was straight from manual 'piano' boards and so the new technology was applied to memorising only the levels of channels which moved from one cue to the next rather than memorising complete cue states. This was also attractive because it required less memory capacity and, in addition to any economic considerations, this saving of memory capacity appealed to the computer world's concept of engineering elegance. In the initial debates about how to apply the new technologies, American users seem to have been rather less involved than their British counterparts. This resulted in European boards talking direct to the stage rather than through a command line as in America. A European keystroke immediately affects the light, whereas an American keystroke is ineffective without a subsequent stroke of the 'Enter' key. These separate operational philosophies remain, although most systems on the market now offer the option of operation in either mode.

The Enter-key option is purely a matter of operator preference, but I normally ask my operator to record the total state of each lighting cue, rather than just the channels moving during the cue change. This is because of the way that I like to take advantage of a memory board's capability to assemble the initial broad outline of the plot quickly, then refine it throughout subsequent rehearsals.

I like to go rather slowly and tentatively with the first few cues; but once confident that the rest of the production team is broadly comfortable with the overall style, and that the palette of lights is actually delivering the anticipated mixes, I accelerate by recording some cues as approximate states. I then return to these for polishing during, or between, later rehearsals when I have the advantage of being able to refine the balance while the actors move.

An approximate state may be derived initially in one of several ways. It is quite likely to be the previous state with only a few prominent channels amended or, if only a subtle change is required, the previous state may be copied unaltered. The rather common 'restore' cue can be made initially by copying an appropriate earlier cue, although every apparently straight restore usually requires more and more fine balancing on each occasion it is seen in rehearsal.

As plotting progresses, there is an increased possibility of using earlier cues as building blocks. Unless I am really up against the clock, I rarely build cues from groups: I like to call each channel individually and see its value. On the other hand, I find groups very useful for removing blocks of lights when plotting a crossfade or check-down. In these circumstances it is very useful to be able to quickly take out, say, all the warm booms or lavender fronts. One 'going-down' device that I never use is the master fader; a general dim seems to generate a muddy look which then takes a lot of internal balancing to get right. It is usually much cleaner to dim a stage by taking some lights out completely, leaving the remaining ones relatively bright.

Even when plotting very fast, I always try to achieve the most accurate cue-timing as possible. Virtually every crossfade requires a different speed for the incoming and outgoing lighting states. Normally, the new state needs to come in quicker so that it is established before the outgoing state drops significantly. Very sophisticated boards allow parts of a cue to be given delayed starts and even a profile of acceleration and deceleration may be recorded. But I find that simple differential timings, such as an incoming state in five seconds and outgoing state in eight seconds usually works fine.

The lights which are tricky, and may need delaying, are the ones which hit scenery and therefore register first, throwing the picture momentarily out of balance. I usually experiment with alternative timings while plotting: even if the cue content is not final, it helps the actors and stage management to have the cue-timings reasonably accurate before the first technical rehearsals. This facilitates clear decisions about whether a timing problem requires addition or subtraction of the odd second, or advancing\delaying of the cue position in the script.

One aspect of timing which can be left until a later phase of rehearsals is the pre-heating of cold lamps to overcome the 'jerk' that may be inserted into a build cue by the delay while lamp filaments warm up. Manufacturers have been surprisingly slow, presumably due to lack of demand, to develop a key stroke that looks at the recorded incoming cue and pre-heats any lamps currently running at zero. However, since the problem usually affects only a few channels in a few cues, it is easy to cheat just enough level into these channels in the previous memory to warm the lamps without generating significant light.

Ideally, at least in theory, all cues would be manually timed by the operator's hand: moving a master-fader as in the old pre-memory days. Subtle variations in actors' timing from one performance to the next are, after all, what makes live-theatre, live! In reality, it's the position of the cue which is likely to vary by a beat or so, rather than the actual running timing of the cue. Furthermore, once the cue has started, any flexibility of timing tends to be closely linked to the predetermined pace of music, sound effects, flying and other scenery movements.

And, finally, unless the production is for a very short run of only three or four performances, there will be a rota of board operators to allow for days off. So, recorded times are the reality of most productions. However, nearly all boards have provision for rapid operator-intervention – to take over instantly, to speed up, slow down or stop the cue.

The techniques we have been discussing are those for a production which is planned, plotted and rehearsed. But how about the 'one night stand' with little or no opportunity for rehearsal? In this situation, lighting design has to be instant with designer–operators responding immediately to stage actions they might not have seen before. In addition, the designer–operator may not have seen the script, any running order may be skeletal and, in the case of a concert, changed as the band respond to their audience. In such circumstances the ultimate test for a good operator is the number which starts so moody that the lighting starts to go smoothly down to a dramatic blue until suddenly, to the surprise of the operator, with a 'hup 2–3–4', the music goes up-tempo. Top operators will slide seamlessly into hot-lighting as if they knew it was going to happen.

In fast design–operation, there is not enough time to call-up memorised states. Instant access is *essential*. Groups or, preferably, balanced states, are pre-loaded on to a series of individual master faders which have associated bump-to-full buttons for flashing. The memories loaded on to these masters will be colour or area groups prepared for the type of show and its stage setting. Alternative memories may be loaded for different scenes, but the fader contents need to accord with a simple logic so that the operator–designer's fingers can locate the appropriate fader without reference to a written plot-sheet. Touch-operation allows concentration on the stage without any need to look at the control desk.

The primary requirement of any control system is *reliability*. Electronic amnesia is not acceptable. Improved belts and braces are more important than additional peripheral function-keys. Aerospace standards are not too high a target for reliability. What about operational priorities thereafter? Well, the prime role of stage technology is to support the actors in performance and, during that performance, operators are akin to actors. This suggests that the operator's needs should take precedence over those of the designer. Fortunately, a board which is operator-friendly tends automatically to be designer-friendly. In a few short years, boards have moved from being stage lighting's most difficult aspect to being its easiest.

Performing dangerously

And now for a dangerous quotation:

"I am all against rehearsal, a most tedious and unnecessary affair. After a very long experience I have discovered that the only way to get a really living and vital performance is not to rehearse it... so that everyone will be struggling hard at the music and that makes a great tension..."

So says Sir Thomas Beecham in *Beecham in Rehearsal*, a record made from an eavesdropping rehearsal tape.

Beecham, of course, did rehearse and his charismatic talent ensured that neither rehearsals or performances were ever tedious. But charisma and talent were only the gloss – the core was *preparation*. His orchestral parts were always carefully marked, and the afternoon between morning rehearsal and evening performance was invariably spent working on these markings. As they turned the pages, his players were liable to find new phrasing indications requiring an instant response from bow or breath. This ensured a performance tension. There could be misses among the hits, but the success rate justified the risk.

Lighting design, like any activity based on creative decision-making, involves taking risks. But lighting designers, like any other artists, can only live dangerously if their preparation is secure. Like a Beecham rehearsal, a lighting rehearsal should avoid tedium by being thoroughly prepared, efficiently conducted, short and *fun*.

7
Lighting
Instruments

My priorities are clear: I would rather have a lamp in an old biscuit box mounted in the right position than the latest all-singing, all-dancing do-everything spotlight in the wrong position. It is the angle at which the light hits the actor or scenic element that is the primary brush stroke in the lighting designer's paintbox.

Assuming that we can place the light in the right position, what next? Brightness is a matter of balance rather than bash, so I tend to place more emphasis on light *quality* rather than on *quantity* when selecting instruments. I am also concerned with being able to make fast adjustments when focusing. Therefore, my first thought in selecting which instrument to use in any particular position is the quality of the light, followed by how well it facilitates speedy adjustments.

The first scribbled squiggles on my scratch pad acknowledge only two kinds of light: parcans and the rest. My friends in the spotlight factories shudder when I claim, as I most certainly do, that the parcan has been the most exciting luminaire development of my lifetime. Yes, halogen lamps are great but, essentially, they are an advance in lighting *management* – we no longer need to continually replace blackened lamps. Why do I love the quality of parcan light? Although softish on the edge, the beam is concentrated, even a little harsh: certainly enough to make a really positive statement with the strong deep colours that I increasingly favour in my old age. It picks up any dirt or moisture in the air to create an enhancing haze around the actor. It is gloriously free from knobs and whistles: up–down, left–right and you've got it. No need to coax the light. Yes, the beam is uneven, but in an interesting way which gives the light an integral chiaroscuro.

With a chorus of parcans (and parcans are so cheap they can be used in mass choir formations) there is usually just enough texture to stop things getting too bland. If the light is too rough for a particular show, it can be smoothed with a diffusion filter. Parcans are the rank-and-file members of the beamlight family whose princesses are the low-voltage parabolic beam-lights. Now, a kilowatt reflected by a parabola – that really makes a positive statement!

Another healthy luminaire development of the last few years has been the rebirth of the simple PC (plano–convex) lens focus-spot. When UK manufacturers gave them up in the late 1950s, I did not mind. After all, the lenses we could afford were rather lousy. PC instruments did carry on in most of the plusher theatres in central Europe – where they could afford better lenses. My memory of the 1950s is of a rather yellow light, edged with the rainbows of chromatic aberration. The glass regularly cracked, with more rainbows appearing down the cracks, and there was even some tendency to project a filament image under certain throw-conditions. By comparison the fresnel gave a white, clean, and smooth light. However, it required a lot of damage-limitation exercises to control the surrounding scatter from the lens. This scatter has become worse in many of the newer fresnels and is the fault of we users who kept pushing the manufacturers to make smaller lights. So they used smaller diameter lenses which are more prone to scatter some light outside the main beam.

The new textured lenses of today's PC focus-spots give a clean, even light with just the right softness of edge for normal work, especially the latest lenses which are clear in the centre but have a perimeter ring which has a diffusing texture. The range of diffusion filters now available allows progressive softening of a plano–convex light until it is equivalent to a fresnel or even softer. But there is no magic filter to put in front of a fresnel to harden its image and reduce its scatter. The way in which these born-again PCs achieve their soft edges, with considerably less scatter than fresnels, has resulted in an accelerating swing towards PCs for many applications. They are certainly a more flexible option for the multi-use stage, making them a more cost-effective investment than fresnels. In some circumstances, the new PCs offer an alternative to profile-spots. Edge quality is very similar to the normal soft-focusing of profile-spots, but smoother across the beam. A single standard instrument covers a wide range of beam angles, and they are free from the blue rings of chromatic aberration which tend to be a by-product of the optical efficiency of the newer profile models. Focusing of the single lens is quicker than a profile's multiple adjustments.

However, profiles do have unique features. Whereas the barndoors of simple PC focus-spots provide only a very rough shaping of the beam, precise shuttering to cast a clean profile gives these spots their name. Gobos allow projection of line images or texturing of the beam. Profiles scatter negligible stray light outside the main beam and are efficient over long throws. Although they will focus to a hard precise image, any such use in the theatre is for an occasional special purpose. Their main deployment is to throw light at a target without any significant light straying sideways on the way.

When a profile's light reaches its target it needs a soft edge because unmotivated hard edges tend to pull the audiences eyes and muddle their perception of the scene. The traditional way to achieve this softening is by throwing the lenses slightly out of focus. But all the adjustments on a profile interact: moving the lens means fiddling with the shutters, probably the lamp-centring knob, possibly an iris and certainly the other lens if it is a variable-beam model. This can be very time consuming, and throwing them out of focus tends to negate some of the benefits gained from computer-aided reflector design. Double edges can appear, often with that dreaded blue ring of chromatic aberration. It is much easier to hard focus: it is quicker and needs little shouted dialogue between lighting designer and focusing technician – focus it hard and then pop a diffuser in.

The full potential of diffusers is just beginning to emerge. I grew up with the traditional frost filters, 29 heavy or 31 light – a heavy that was too heavy and a light that was not light enough. In the fifties, I caught the last of the gelatine filters and I remember the old operators of perch arcs using drops of oil to clarify the diffusion in the centre of their frosts. In the early sixties I found glass directional diffusers being used in Europe (although not in Britain), particularly to elongate side lighting in the vertical plane. But, in general, the diffusers of my youth were rather specialised devices. Fine for smoothing-out the colour joins from short-throw floods on cycloramas and for putting softly decorative blobs on scenery, but normally too rough for acting areas. Our need is to diffuse the light just enough to soften it, but in doing so, throw out absolutely minimal scatter.

Any diffuser has to be assessed according to two major lighting *design* parameters:

- What the diffuser does to the beam, particularly its edge.

- The scatter that the diffuser generates adjacent to the emerging beam.

In addition, there is one major lighting *management* parameter:

- How much focus-time is saved by using diffuser filters rather than adjusting the optical system?

In general, the longer the throw, the more critical is the delicacy of the diffuser required. When Hamburg frost arrived more that a decade or so ago, it provided a viable technique for shorter throws – particularly cross-lighting from the wings. Then half-Hamburg made the technique viable on longer throws from overhead and from auditorium positions close to the proscenium arch. But even half-Hamburg is too strong for longer throws, particularly from side wall positions with the risk of light flaring on to the walls. However there are quality control problems in manufacturing a quarter-Hamburg: it is really quite a problem to maintain consistency when making something that is so close to clear.

The use of discharge lamps is increasing and this is a trend which will continue and probably accelerate in two areas: for the long throws of big venues and the growing use of lighting styles based on a few huge lamps making big directional statements. This is an area where fresnels are still king. HMIs are definitely not a suitable lamp for jumbo-PCs softened with melting frosts. However, as we move towards these jumbo lights, it is appropriate to recall something that the late Howard Bay, for so long a leading and innovative American set and lighting designer said to me at a time when five kilowatt was the biggest light we could consider. He said:

"Give a theatre one 5K but one only. One gives a strong directional beam. But if there is a second it is likely to get used to balance the first one and so the whole light will escalate in brightness. Uniform brightness. The irises in the audience's eyes will close up and we will be back where we started, but with extra strain on the air conditioning."

Brightness is about balance. I have no craving for more lights or for lights with more sophisticated shutters. But I do dream of more, and easier, control of light quality. I fantasise about controls which would allow the texture across the beam to be varied subtly, while the edge remained positive yet soft and totally free from scatter. Waiting for technology to provide wish-fulfilment, I have my break-up gobos and diffusers – the technology may be low but the contribution to the light palette is high.

Collectives

Sheep flock and cows herd. You can have a swarm of bees, a school of porpoises or a pack of wolves. But how about light-persons? Perhaps a lumen of lighters? Well, Alan Ayckbourne is thought to be the first person to have referred to a gobo of lighting designers.

Saintly light

Lighting designers are not particularly renowned for their saintly habits. But it would appear that they have at least two saints to inspire their labours. As Bernard Levin once put it in a rather devastating opera review: "The lighting appeared to be the fruit of an alliance between St. Dunstan and St. Vitus."

Ei blot til lyst

'Not for pleasure only' is the message over the proscenium arch in Copenhagen's *Royal Theatre*. Many theatre performances are 'for pleasure only' and some could be labelled 'not for pleasure'. But the best have a subtlety that involves pleasure but goes beyond: the Danes inscribed a fundamental truth on their proscenium when building this theatre in 1875.

8

Integrating With Auditorium Architecture

My belief that the most critical design factor is the angle at which light hits the actors and\or scene results in considerable agonising about where to put the lights. In a studio space with an all-over modular grid, the choice of positions is virtually unlimited. In most theatres, however, ideals have to modified to use the restricted positions available. Backstage restrictions are dependent upon scenery needs but the compromise for each production is subject to discussion. These limitations may be considerable, especially with a scenically-heavy show, but they are nothing compared with the restrictions usually imposed by the auditorium architecture.

However, it would be unrealistic to deny that a few restrictions can be something of a relief. Although they do force one's hand, limitation of choice can be a stimulating antidote to the terror of a blank sheet with its offer of unlimited possibilities. Drawing the permanent FOH (front of house) lights on a plan can really encourage me to believe that I have made some progress with my design. The achievement may be illusory, but I work in the illusion business! We cannot expect theatres built in the days of candles, oil, gas, or in the early years of electricity to have proper provision for mounting spotlights in the auditorium. But we should be able to have a reasonable expectation of increasingly effective FOH positions in those built during the second-half of our century. Alas, there is no certainty of this and, in a curious inversion of the way things usually are, the situation got better before it got worse.

The theatres of the turn of the century have high ceilings which are usually so far above the top of the proscenium arch that any spotlights mounted in them would provide only a vertical angle too close to downlight for eyes and teeth. However, the balcony fronts of such theatres usually provide a series of alternative frontal angles. The quality of side-lighting is highly dependent upon the positioning of the boxes adjacent to the proscenium, particularly when they are adorned with fantasies of ornate plaster which stop beams reaching into their own side of the stage.

In response to the democratic sightlines of the cinema, later theatres were built with a single low balcony with a front which provides an angle so close to horizontal that actor high shadows are inevitable. The ceiling is usually too high, but angled sidewalls provide an opportunity for useful booms. However, I would like to see the Broadway practice of placing hi-hats on the front of every side-FOH instrument being adopted as an international standard. Not just to contain the spill but to reduce the likelihood of the audience catching sight of the colour frame out of the corner of their eye.

The dilemma in old theatres is one of *conservation*. Early spotlight incursions into the auditorium were disguised by discreet modifications, particularly the addition to gallery fronts of boxes with plasterwork in the style of the original fascia. But FOH lighting has grown to a point where the numbers are just too large to hide. Many of these theatres are so beautiful that no one would deny that modern lighting equipment is an ugly intrusion. But can we seriously reduce production standards in a theatre in order to preserve the original auditorium ambience while the audience are assembling?

Debate inevitably arises when an old theatre is being restored or refurbished. The architects, quite naturally, hope to minimise the intrusion of technical equipment. Although it is highly likely that the consultants were once technicians, time tends to have distanced them from the hard realities of the staging process.

Given their close working relationship with the architects and the need to satisfy clients who do not wish their heritage disfigured, it is perhaps understandable that the consultants tend to agree that everything will be fine provided the lighting designers exercise some discipline. So, for example, they may agree to omit provision for hanging an advance bar above the orchestra pit-rail – not even arranging for neatly grommeted holes to be inserted in the ceiling while the scaffolding is still up. Before long, a touring company makes its appearance conditional upon the availability of an advance bar. So, early one Sunday morning, ugly ceiling holes get hastily knocked-through from the roof void. It is inevitable that any extra bars which sprout in the auditorium are uglier than if they had been planned as an integral feature. However, new technologies offer a solution: remotely focusable spots with colour-scrollers can reduce the number of instruments in each position, although not the number of positions.

The immediate post-war decades of theatre building adopted an auditorium format that was particularly receptive to lighting integration. With the aim of reducing the framing effect of the proscenium, every effort was made to ensure that the join between the stage and the fashionable wedge-shaped auditorium was as unstressed as possible. There was no structural proscenium arch: the stage began at the natural termination of the sloping ceiling and curving walls. Such a ceiling was ideally placed for lighting bridges which could be harmoniously integrated within the roof void and provide good lighting angles. Similarly, the curve of the walls could be interrupted to form side lighting slots with rear access ladders incorporated within the wall structure. With at least two bridges and two sets of slots, all judiciously located, FOH lighting in these theatres reached, and still enjoys, the peak of its development for fast focus from good positions.

Alas, the raked wedge has been found to be relatively unsatisfactory as the shape for an auditorium, particularly when the capacity increases above about 400 seats. It does provide excellent sightlines but, in doing this, tends to isolate individuals so that they do not gel into an audience who respond as a corporate whole. Moreover, it is such a space-hungry format that the rear seating extends to an unacceptable distance from the stage. Consequently there has been a return to the traditional format where the audience hang on the walls, enjoying close contact with the stage even if they have a less than complete line of sight. Peopled walls increase the intimacy of an auditorium, helping the audience to unite in their relationship with the actors. This is, understandably, most apparent in audience reaction to a comedy.

As a result of this architectural development, some of the old FOH lighting problems have returned. However, in many respects the situation is much better than with the historic theatres. Ceilings remain low and can therefore be designed to incorporate good lighting bridges. But the reintroduction of audience seating on the side walls reduces, and in most cases removes, the possibility of vertical lighting slots. So we become dependent upon finding good positions for horizontal bars at several levels. There is no universal solution to this but it does require the provision to be made as an integral part of the auditorium design concept, not grafted on at the detailing phase. This should not be a problem because, although modern spotlights may look visually uncomfortable amidst nineteenth century gilded plaster, they are acceptable, even expected, in most of today's auditorium styles.

I make no apology for stressing the need for good FOH rigging positions. Provided that the backstage area provides a reasonably wide, deep and most importantly, a *clear* space with good suspension facilities, all we need is decent FOH positions to ensure that light can fulfil its dramatic potential. Although most of the light is likely to be required at angles from about 30° above the horizontal to about 30° less than the vertical, some provision needs to be available from all angles, particularly from the near horizontal and, if possible, from below the horizontal. Perhaps the neatest and, most cost-effective provision for occasionally used angles is that at Basildon Towngate Theatre where short lengths of painted scaffolding-bar are incorporated into the decorative treatment of all the balcony fronts, with hinged sections of the padded leaners allowing concealed temporary cabling.

FOH light tends to be unloved, often regarded as something best avoided or at least treated as a necessary evil. The major discrediting factor is the flattening effect, and there can also be dislike of the extent to which the lighting level within the auditorium increases. Both of these are largely historical. The levels of today's on-stage lighting are sufficiently high to bounce out into the auditorium, lighting it up irrespective of the

FOH. Which is fine because we have rediscovered the importance of treating stage and auditorium as a single room and this is assisted by light, provided the balance overwhelmingly favours the stage. Flatness is trickier but again it is a matter of balance. FOH gained its reputation for flatness in the days when downlight and backlight were virtually unknown and sidelight was discreet almost to the point of being vestigial. Now that we use them as the major source for modelling and colouring, frontlight can be raised to a sufficient level for facial clarity and eye sparkle.

But the angle is critical. So, on making my first visit to any theatre, after absorbing the total ambience, the first technical details I look at are the FOH positions.

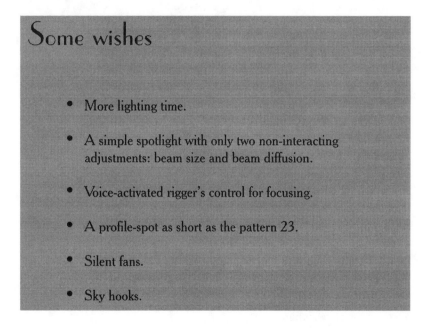

Some wishes

- More lighting time.

- A simple spotlight with only two non-interacting adjustments: beam size and beam diffusion.

- Voice-activated rigger's control for focusing.

- A profile-spot as short as the pattern 23.

- Silent fans.

- Sky hooks.

9
Filtering
Light

Changing fashions are a major influence on the use of colour. Some fashions, particularly those derived from strong convictions about the nature and purpose of drama, are capable of provoking an emotive response of considerable strength, particularly among directors. However, it is perhaps not surprising that coloured light should be regarded with some suspicion: it is, after all, light from which important parts have been removed. Indeed, coloured light is regarded as unclean to such an extent by some of the more doctrinaire enthusiasts of dramatic purity, that only unfiltered 'white' light is considered suitable to illuminate the 'truth' in the playwright's text.

One of the more enduring fashionable options of recent years has been to cover the stage with an all pervading evenly bright light from visible sources, all at maximum intensity and without filters. In occasional moments of cynicism, I sometimes wonder whether this, like much of the other theoretical underpinning of late twentieth-century staging, may be the result of some wag substituting Brecht one-liners for the more traditional mottos in a box of christmas crackers at a nineteen-fifties dinner party. Conversations with technicians at Berlin's *Theater am Schiffbau-erdamm* in the mid-seventies revealed that Brecht had not been averse to dimming individual lights below maximum intensity in order to balance the picture. Lighting cues were not unknown, and his light was normally filtered to enhance its clarity. Brecht had doubtless shared my own experience of seeing our grandmothers add a 'blue bag' dye to the weekly wash to ensure the whiter than white which is central to every detergent manufacturer's marketing strategy and is achieved by the same blue method.

Although I myself have never been a white-lighter, I did get caught up in the fall-out from the surge of 'open-white' from lights with no filter. I remember telling my RADA students in the 1960s to "Think of open-white as normal and only add a colour if you have a definite reason for doing so." I think this advice probably stemmed from subconscious guilt. Not just guilt that I continued to use colour at a time when the more crusading members of my generation were forging a new, seemingly wondrous, monochromatic theatre, but also guilt that I popped filters into all my lights for no other reason than I took a fancy to certain colours in the swatch book of samples. Apart from two open-white shows which were an unspeakably depressing experience, the only time that any light of mine has been filter free is when I have removed a filter to get a bit more light. If I want monochromatic light, I filter with a hint of blue–grey, in the spirit of Brecht and his grandmama.

However, whether involved as audience or as designer, I cannot claim that this is a production style which engages my sympathy. Whilst not denying the power of drama to engage the intellect in a debate of ideas, I derive more exciting stimulation from the potential of theatre as a medium for the exploration of emotions. In such a theatre, colour is a powerful tool, particularly when deployed to assist in exerting a subconscious influence on the audience. One of the fascinations of theatre is that people, who would be outraged by any proposal that subliminal suggestion might be used for advertising or political purposes, cheerfully pay for a ticket which effectively sanctions an attempt to tamper with the subconscious recesses of their minds.

Colour has a delicate but intriguing role to play in this process. Does each tint have an inherent emotional meaning? Or does colour-response depend on conditioning by a series of colour experiences starting with baby clothes and continuing through such stimuli as poems and songs about the moon? Can we influence audience response by reinforcing, or even establishing, the emotional significance of particular colours early in a play in order to enhance their contribution to the climax? My observations indicate that audience response involves all three factors. However, the contribution of each is very difficult to quantify, if only because of the wide range of sensitivity between individual people.

The clearest, simplest and most universally recognised connection (at least, in the western world) between coloured light and emotion seems to lie in the range from warm–happy through neutral to cool–sad. This is a continuous scale which has no definitive points because response to colour is relative. Whether the light on one part of the stage is perceived as cool or warm will depend on comparison with the colour of light on another part of the stage or in an immediately prior cue sequence. But this is only one of the factors affecting filter choice. The light on an actor or piece of scenery is the cumulative effect of several sources: there is likely to be an overlay of several beams plus reflected light which has been affected by the colour of the reflecting surfaces. Some difference in the colour from identical filters, particularly paler filters, will arise from the reddening effect when a lamp filament is dimmed.

These psychological and practical factors make the consequences of filter choice difficult to predict. It is therefore one of the more agonising areas of lighting-design decision. This makes the white-light option an attractive alternative and it is not difficult to fantasise that Brecht may just possibly have rationalised an urge, in the midst of some long forgotten endless lighting session in his youth, to shout "Stop, stop, forget it – let's just put everything up to full and get on with the rehearsal or we'll never get to the pub."

My own filter philosophy is simple. Colour can support and enhance the work of the actors, their clothes and their scenic environment. When I use filters, I may be removing some parts of the light but I am enhancing the power of those that remain. I am aware that my audience like myself, watch a lot of television and so I must light to produce much more natural skin tones than I did twenty years ago. My colour ambience now has to surround the actor, tinting the environment, particularly the airspace that the light passes through and the floor that it hits, while leaving face and costume as naturally coloured as possible. The practicalities of this are based on a realisation that if I take the spectrum apart with filters, then I can put that spectrum together again by superimposing the filtered light beams. It is gloriously unscientific: not so much a rule-of-thumb as one of crossed fingers.

New technology, however, is taking some of the agony out of filter choice. Scrollers allow us to increase our colour options for each light, while Vari*Lite has opened the way to instant choice of virtually any colour without pre-planning. Scrollers are established, although I admit to some doubt when saw the prototype of their microprocessor selection from a roll of tape-joined filters driven by a whizzingly-fast motor. But their popularity is testimony to their accuracy. Vari*Lite, and its clones, use colour like paint. With motorised dichroic filters inside the spotlight, the mixing possibilities are virtually unlimited: not only is there is no need to think of filter numbers but it can be inhibiting to do so.

But most of the time, we just have to commit at the drawing board to one filter for each light. I find it difficult to be scientific about the choice. It is a mix of experience and experiment. I still shine coloured light experimentally to see what happens. Firstly on to the designs, then on to the frocks, flesh and paint. In doing so, I take comfort from the knowledge that, even when using the deepest colours, I am moving towards neutrality by reassembling the spectrum as I pile on the colour beams.

Moon watching

I have passed a lot of my life, particularly my operatic life, by stage moonlight – that atmospheric moonshine which conveniently waxes and wanes on cue, casting its moonbeams into dramatically appropriate corners with a fine disregard for the sciences of astronomy and mete-orology. So, every year, I set aside fourteen consecutive nights for the observation of the real thing. Selecting a suitable mediterranean seascape, I take a serious look at this nocturnal primary source with the concentration that any audience is entitled to expect from their lighting designer.

At the merest indication on the horizon of a possible entrance, the cork is pulled. For midsummer moonwatching, something very dry, very chilled is advised for starters, possibly progressing to something red and mellow as the night matures. The first appearance is often tinged with a positive gold: 47 or even 34 – I still think in the old basic cinemoid colours even if my final choice is translated into the subtler options of the modern swatches. The beam is tightly-parallel as from a true par-abolic reflector – although I do not recall mission control reporting that the man in the moon has a parabolic countenance.

Mr Moon soon becomes a follow-spot whose phosphorescence tingles over the ripples with unerring aim as a I tramp along the beach. Then a colour modulation through 52, open-white, 17 and finally 61. The skyward track is accompanied by a slight distortion of source to produce a gently conical beam. There are subtle nightly variations as in all good live shows, but a standard reference is provided by the precisely-shaped, focused and timed beam from the lighthouse. When spot has opened to full-flood I take to my bed, knowing that the remains of the nightly lunar progress will not yet have settled behind the mountains by the first swim and gin of the morrow.

10
Looking
Back

In the stage lighting business, as in every other business, there is a happy band – or perhaps not-so-happy band – to whom nothing is new or exciting. They are the 'seen-it-all-befores'. "What about the boxed limes in *Kitchen Koncerto!*" we enthuse. "Old stuff," they reply, "Willy Bungle used them in 1923 for the first act finale of *Gavottes from Old Ambrosia.*" "Computer-designed reflectors!" they snort contemptuously, "Issy De Cee calculated every reflector facet of his 1912 fly flood on a bead frame."

How important is the history of stage lighting? Much lip service is paid to the study of history: only by consideration of the past are we supposed to be able to predict and control our future destiny. One does not need a doctorate in cynicism to question the success of this theory in the fields of economics and politics. Is stage lighting any different? At school, I rejected history as irrelevant – an attitude maintained until my forties when I realised that the people who mutter about the degeneracy of modern youth were no longer referring to me. Suddenly, history came alive! – I had become part of it. Now resting on museum shelves are the very dimmers and lamps that I once used to light shows. Coming to terms with my own past, I began to realise the importance of the days of lighting yore.

Although history can be fascinating in its own right, its positive value lies in the proposition: *to move forward, first look back.* Is there anything in the old technology and the way it was used that can stimulate our current and future thinking? Reconsidering yesterday's equipment is much easier than discovering how it was used.

Documentation allows us a reasonably accurate visualisation of how the scenery and costumes looked under working light. But how did they look under production lighting? It is very difficult to establish what the lighting intent was, and how well it was realised.

The graphics of scene and costume design are pictorial. Drawings, paintings and models prepared by scenery and costume designers offer a visual statement of how the production is intended to look. Photographs and videos of performance provide a reasonably accurate record of how the designs were realised. But the graphics of lighting design are diagrammatic. The plan prepared by a lighting designer indicates the positioning of each lighting instrument, its type, colour filter and control channel. This plan is supported by schedules of instrument focusing, intended composition of each picture and proposed timing of changes from one picture to the next. But, except in rare cases where the scenography team prepare a detailed storyboard with an impression of light and shade included, there is no visual representation of lighting intent.

Visual records of how the production actually looked in performance are misleading because photographs record frozen moments of a dynamic light which is constantly fluid whether the light is changing or whether actors are moving within a static light-balance. While video recording does include the time dimension, all visual recording methods provide a misleading picture of how the light actually looked because both emulsion photography and digital recording tends to exaggerate contrast. Consequently, lighting documentation, when it exists, cannot be interpreted with any acceptable degree of accuracy, even by experienced lighting designers. Furthermore, any interpretation is extremely difficult to communicate to anyone who does not have similar experience in lighting design.

If we believe that history can be helpful, we need to become more methodical in our preservation of equipment and documents, adopting a magpie mentality to items such as cables, catalogues, clamps, controls, correspondence, data sheets, dimmers, ephemera, filters, floods, gobos, invoices, irises, lamps, lenses, lighting designs, memos, optical effects, patch panels, photographs, plans, plots, plugs, prototypes, quotations, reminiscences, research and development files, shutters, sockets, spots, stencils, tenders, theses, transparencies, working drawings, and all kinds of accessories.

There have been many discussions about the possibility of a *museum of theatre technology* where historical equipment could be displayed, and, as far as possible, restored to working order. Locating such a museum in an old theatre would allow each type of equipment to be exhibited in its specialised environment. However, to facilitate lighting research, perhaps a resource centre dedicated solely to lighting would be more advantageous. Assembling a wide range of yesterday's equipment alongside today's would enable research to take place under the laboratory conditions appropriate to a subject that is so acutely at the interface of art and science. While there are certainly emotional reasons for locating in a old theatre, a redundant church might provide more practical accommodation.

Since today's innovations become tomorrow's history, perhaps we should be rather more systematic in preserving documentation of our own productions for future analysis. But, in view of the problems already noted in respect of the diagrammatic nature of lighting graphics and the difficulties of recording performance lighting, the starting point for serious research would seem to be a study of archival methods. Traditional documentation will remain, but developing technologies offer many new possibilities. Computer-aided design is already generating information in digital form for compact storage and rapid access. Computer visualisation has demonstrated considerable development potential as an exciting new tool for the process of lighting design, generating a pictorial representation of intent in an easily-filed digital format. The only difficulty that stands in the way of a systematic approach to lighting archives is, as always, *money*. Meanwhile, a few dedicated enthusiasts are preserving key archaeological remains in their barns, lofts and even under their beds.

What lessons might we learn from the past? Let me take a personal glance backwards. Throughout my life, new technology has had an enabling effect on the work of the lighting designer. The fundamentals are still the same, but new technology tends to make them much easier to implement. In my lifetime the thyristor dimmer was perhaps the second biggest revolution, with memory desks being, of course, the big one! These are things which we now take for granted, but there are less obvious control improvements such as multiplexing – which banished millions of wires at a stroke. Of all the knobs and whistles added to control desks in the last few years, which is the most important? The one we are already wondering how we ever did without? I suggest soft-patching. Other key developments? Halogen lamps put a stop to shows going on a slow fade to black from the moment they were lamped. They lengthened lamp-life so that no longer are we unlikely to get through a dress rehearsal or first night without a critical light blowing. Then there was the simple elegance of the humble hook-clamp which, overnight, replaced all its complex ancestors.

These are all enabling devices which have allowed lighting design to become more adventurous and efficient. This had a considerable effect on the quality of lighting because, although extended sequences of precise cues had always been possible, operation required many pairs of hands and many hours of rehearsal. However, there are developments which have had a fundamental effect on the look of our stage. I would suggest that the key ones are gobos, parcans, discharge lamps and diffusers.

But, as we try to take lighting forward, are there any areas of abandoned technology that we might reconsider? How about the foot-pushes of the light console? These were mainly a doubling-up of hand controls for use when the operator ran out of fingers. Fingers may no longer be a problem, but the unique feature was the foot pedal which set the cue speed. Most operators are car drivers for whom the movement of an accelerator is the most natural form of speed control. The light console's balanced pedal actually set the speed, but a memory control might find more use for a pedal to override memorised timings. Foot-down to speed up, shift the pressure to the heel to raise the pedal for slowing down. Also, there might possibly be a role for the feet when lighting controls expand to include handling all the movements of remotely-focusable lights in addition to intensity. Staying with feet, how about the footlights which were, for so long, not only an indispensable light source but virtually an icon for 'theatre'? They were hounded out for reasons that were valid at the time but bear reassessment now. Footlights were dismissed mainly because the angle of their light was unnatural. It was unflattering on the actors and threw multiple rising-shadows of them on to the scenery. Footlights were also considered to be a barrier between actor and audience; although this rather academic argument seems to have held little sway – either with the actors or their audience. Concern about the lighting angle failed to identify the problem as one of balance. Whereas footlights as a major light source are an effect to be used only for a very positive reason, a small proportion of soft light from below is very helpful in correcting some of the hard face-shadows from overhead sources.

Actors, especially in comedy, have found footlights to be supportive and comforting – even welcoming the slight feeling of 'barrier'. Many theoreticians may find it difficult to understand but some actors, particularly those who appear to establish a very close relationship with their audience, suffer from a fear of that very same audience; footlights afford the illusion of protection. It is interesting to observe the number of tiny 'birdie' spotlights currently sprouting along the front edge of the stage in many productions. Although new lamps would permit a very compact unit, any serious return to footlighting would require restoration of the sloping troughs which were once a feature of the front of every stage to ensure that the footlights did not interfere with the sightlines.

With simple plano–convex focus spotlights successfully revived, there may not be much scope for looking backwards into old spotlight technology. However, there has never really been a proper replacement for the pattern 23. Although it has been overtaken in optical performance, few of today's baby-spots have the resilience of this tough little die-cast survivor, and none of them have its short back-to-front dimension which allows it to point upstage without fouling flown scenery in a tightly hanging rig.

The twin lenses of zoom profile-spots move independently to permit variations in both the size of the beam and the quality of its edge. The interaction requires considerable to-ing and fro-ing between lenses when focusing. Yet one of the earliest zoom profiles and the first follow-spot to use a compact source iodine discharge lamp, the Strand Pattern 265, had its lenses coupled. There could be considerable attraction in a coupled zoom-spot where the edge quality was preset as slightly soft but with the option of decoupling to sharpen when required.

Another technique that might bear re-examination is the bifocal twin shutter sets of the Pattern 264 and 764. Beyond the normal gate shutters and, therefore, slightly away from the optical centre, the second set of shutters, with serrated edges, provided soft edges without disturbing the hard-edge position of the lens. Although a mixture of hard and soft edges was possible, these instruments were normally used with four soft edges. When twin lens profiles were developed, double-shuttering seemed cumbersome and unnecessary. So the old was abandoned in the inevitable flush of enthusiasm for the new. Worth reconsidering, perhaps even in association with coupled-zooming? All today's shutters are sliders with successful operation dependent upon a critical amount of friction which is balanced between jamming and slipping. Rumour has it that the shutters of early Leko prototypes had a screw mechanism.

High-intensity discharge lamps have opened up new possibilities for slide projection. Perhaps it is time to re-examine Linnebach shadow-projection techniques with a view to taking advantage of discharge lamps which are not only brighter but have an option of being closer to a point source than the tungsten lamps originally used.

Turning to the influence of technology on lighting design techniques, it would be interesting to research the extent to which current procedures are influenced, possibly even inhibited, by restrictions of old technology. How much has American design been influenced by early restrictions of patching to a small number of dimmers, in contrast to the long-established European practice of dimmer-per-channel? Has European design been affected by the timing restrictions of electromagnetic servo boards? How have the restrictions and benefits of the repertoire system influenced lighting in central Europe?

Perhaps it would be interesting to re-examine the limitless space of the full cyclorama dome which curved around and above the acting area. This would stimulate a re-examination of psychologically-based colour washing and the concept of softly diffused, all-pervading light which was prevalent in the nineteen-thirties. The importance of such reconsiderations of the past does not lie so much in the limited possibility of rediscovering neglected techniques or ideas, but in the stimulation of looking afresh at things that people were trying to do but were thwarted by the technology, and possibly even the attitudes, of their time.

Ring up the tabs

I took my wife to the theatre last night. "Look," she said, "the tabs are in." She was once a stage manager and so she talks about the tabs being in rather than the curtain being down. And, indeed, the curtain *was* down – rich folds of scarlet plush softly lit by a pair of barndoored fresnels in a strong pink. Alas, no footlights, for uplight is the only truly magical mystery tab warmer. But mystery enough. What lies behind these tabs? What will be revealed when they are flown out? I grow all warm and cosy with anticipation.

This is a rare pleasure because house-tabs seem to have fallen into disgrace: a device only to be used by the truly avant-garde or by an occasional mature director with a concern for sensual pleasures rather than intellectual fashions. Exposing the stage setting to the view of an arriving audience has become the norm. Surely not a fear that too much anticipation might breed anticlimax? Perhaps a gentle preparation for scenery that has become representational to the point of being vestigial? So we are usually required to sit and stare at an expensive surround that does not quite mask. If it is an itchy play, some of the Equity members may already be scratching themselves in carefully rehearsed casual poses – at a time when everyone knows that they should be in their dressing rooms preparing to face us by downing a stiff gin!

But last night was magic. As live chords leaped from the pit, the houselights dimmed to half, holding their final fade until they could glide to nothing on a sinuous oboe entry. The tab dressing-fade was timed precisely so that the rise of the tabs was an exact follow-on to the blackout. The goboed stage was empty for one breath-catching second before the actors appeared as the front-of-house lighting curved softly in. Before hearing one word, we were hooked.

11
Looking
Forward

Market research is a relatively new concept for the theatre-lighting industry. There was little point in analysing user requirements in any significant detail until technology had advanced to a point where it became possible to specify the operationally desirable rather than just the technically possible. But with science developing the potential to be a true servant of art, it has become increasingly necessary for the scientists to ask the artists to specify their ideal palette. There must, of course, be a debate. The scientists still need to share their discoveries with the artists. The possible can be a powerful stimulant of the desirable. But the debate needs *structure* – most decisions of a theatrical nature are made in a climate of expediency. Consequently, the operational philosophy of an articulate customer, waving a megabucks contract for a prestigious theatre, has been known to influence a whole generation of control systems. Any market research has tended to be of an empirical kind and carried out mainly at trade fairs.

- **Method one** ('me too') is to check out what each competitor is doing and incorporate every one of these ideas.

- **Method two** ('you wannit, you gotit') is to give equal credence to everyone who sits down at a control desk with the sole object of discovering what it will not do.

From time to time, everyone looks in their crystal ball. What do I see in mine? How will tomorrow's technology affect our stage lighting ideas and the way we implement them? How can user interact with maker to ensure that it is the theatre *performance* that benefits?

As we move towards a new century, how will theatre lighting develop? What should we be trying to do, and how might technology enable us to do it? We need to consider these questions from the viewpoints of both lighting design and lighting management. So let us look at a few areas of developing technology. Where shall we start? What is the big one – the one with most potential to change our lighting lives? I guess it could be the wonders of remote-controlled lighting instruments. Personally, I don't like the 'intelligent lights' label which has been gaining some currency. I don't want a light with a mind of its own, I want *obedient lights* that do what they are told! This is an area of exciting new technology that is already here today, with the promise of much more excitement still to come. What we have seen so far is only the beginning; there is potential for a future in which light can make an ever more positive contribution to the art of the theatre.

But this future also holds much that can frighten any actor, director, choreographer, set and costume designer, and, yes, frighten me. Imagine the possibility of some mad light-person, eyes ablaze with numbers, dichroics, servos and protocols, turning performances into crazy ballets of dancing lights which distract from the human performers. Whatever our image of this mad light-person, whether it be the demon organist with fingers poised above the keyboard, ready to unleash a concerto of passionate dynamics, or the cool, controlled logic of intergalactic mission control where decisions are made with all the icy passion of the psychiatrist's couch, the thought that one person could have so much control of so much light movement is not comforting.

Of course, I exaggerate. But we must surely always be aware of the dangers that, when we develop a technology to give us more control, we might just create something that we cannot handle. Indeed, we already see some problems in our use of new lighting technology. Already, in many sectors of entertainment, lighting equipment is being used to create effects simply because the equipment has a particular effect-capability, irrespective of whether that effect will support and enhance the performance.

The warning comes clearest from the world of pop–rock where flashing and chasing has become such a routine response that it no longer has very much meaning. Indeed, it is often only when the lights *stop* flickering that they make a positive visual statement. There are some signs of the same situation already happening in the use of remotely-controlled spotlights. Their programming possibilities are indeed wonderful and virtually unlimited. But so many of the sequences we see – sequences which we are assured have been precisely programmed – all too often look like random, mindless movements. Almost as if the designer and the operator had been replaced by a random-number generator.

So, having alerted ourselves to the potential dangers, how can we use this wonderful new technology to advance the art and craft of performance? Design, any design, is a process of decision making. All designers have to make creative decisions and management decisions. Remote-control luminaires offer wonderful new possibilities, both for managing light and for designing a light which makes a real contribution to the performance. The creative decisions and the management decisions are not separate but influence each other. Since they interact so very positively, we must consider their impact separately and together.

Firstly, consider the possible effect of remote-controlled lights on lighting *management*. The removal of the need for access to lights for focusing brings the possibility of new efficiency. Remotely-focused lights are not new, nor is the capability to memorise the focusing data. But until quite recently their repeat accuracy – their ability to return to exactly the same position, time-after-time – was sufficiently accurate only for backlighting. But today, a spotlight can repeat-focus itself as accurately as the finest technician can do it, and much faster than any technician can do it because the spotlight carries out all adjustments simultaneously. It is not possible for a pair of human hands to adjust, pan, tilt, lens, iris and colour all at the same time. But it is easy for a computer. So, to some extent spelling out the obvious, we can look to see some major changes in lighting management – a phased, but increasing, sequence of changes – in the following areas:

- In older theatres, the auditorium architecture cannot accommodate many lights, and the positions which are available often have access problems. Remote focusing during the performance requires a smaller number of instruments, with access required for maintenance only.

- Above the stage, access to lights for focusing is not only time consuming, it is often very difficult, if not impossible, due to the position of scenery. The accuracy of the new lights permits the remote techniques that have been previously used only for backlights to be extended to other parts of the stage.

- In repertoire, which in the UK and USA is restricted mainly to opera and dance but in Europe includes the majority of theatre of all kinds, there is a possibility of hanging temporary lights for one performance only, using flying lines which are for lights tonight but may be for scenery yesterday and tomorrow.

- When touring, where traditional technology has already benefited from experience of the fast-rigging techniques of rock-and-roll, a castored length of truss, complete with remote spotlights, can be wheeled from a truck, flown and plugged. After the computer has run a self-check and reported any problems, the lights will set themselves for the first scene and be ready to refocus themselves as many times as needed during the performance in accordance with instructions from the data stored in the control system.

- One-night-stands, when there is just no time to focus from ladders, can now have something more than just general washes of light.

All this is one of the biggest breakthroughs in stage-lighting technology since gas replaced oil and candles. Money will, of course, be the major factor in the speed of the revolution. But I believe that increasing use of this technology will demonstrate effective capital investment for reducing running costs. Remote control of lights will continue to develop because operation by hand will become too expensive – both in time and money. Improvements in safe working procedures are another important factor as the regulators and insurers become increasingly concerned with the operational risks involved in using ladders and mobile access-towers.

The advantages for lighting *management* are clear, but will this technology produce better lighting? What new creative possibilities are offered for lighting *design*? In discussing the management of lighting, our main concern was the possibilities which come from focusing without access to the spotlight, and then memorising that focus for an accurate repeat whenever required.

In lighting design, we are concerned with the dynamic effect of a moving light-beam and the possibility of using light in ways that increasingly approach the techniques of the painter. Control of the light beam can now come directly under the hands of the light-painter. Over the years there has been much talk, usually of a rather romantic nature, about 'painting with light'. However, the traditional language of theatre lighting is not a visual one – it is *numbers*. Numbers for channels, numbers for dimmers, numbers for colour filters, percentage numbers for brightness levels and numbers for memories. The latest developments in control surfaces – surfaces which act as the human–machine interface, seek a more direct, hands-on approach rather than the traditional conversion of requirements into numbers for access through such conventional devices as levers, wheels and keypads.

The technology of computer-based graphic design allows a lighting operator to convert directly from a plan which can be laid out in any desired format. This may be the geography of the stage, a sketched drawing, a list, anything – perhaps even a storyboard. We are close to CAD–CAM if we want to go that way (CAM stands for computer-aided manufacture). The digitisers available as optional control surfaces for lighting boards are basically the same as those on computers used for lighting design. So we have the possibility of using a direct 'hands-on' approach to playing all functions of the light – even if this implies the dangers, mentioned earlier, of megalomania a-la organ gallery or mission control. The best way will take time to evolve. But we have that time available because this full playability only becomes feasible when most of our lights have become remotes.

But when using only a few remotes, and getting to know their possibilities, we are likely to need to use, during rehearsals, a movement-control desk which is separate from the intensity-control desk with the lighting designer talking, with verbal requests, to individual operators. Once the production has been plotted and rehearsed, all control functions may be brought together for performance under a single operator, either on an integrated control or by the main control sending a pulse to its slave.

Many theatres will doubtless continue to operate in this way, but the options will be almost limitless. Not only do various types of graphic style control surfaces allow an approach which has more in common with painting rather than engineering, but there is the possibility of direct linkage to the ever-developing computer software for designing light, so that a lighting designer's studio becomes capable not only of computer-aided design but computer-aided manufacture (CAM).

Inevitably, there will be some reaction against all this. Theatre is full of cycles of action and reaction. People are always saying "Let's get back to basics..., back to a simple theatre..., street theatre..., all we need is a simple platform and a *passion*!" Then, as they become more successful, they have to re-invent the conventional theatre with all its technology. Until somebody else reacts and the whole cycle starts again. So, there will always be simple theatres where simple lights are focused from ladders. And I, for one, shall enjoy working in them. But, in the main, new technology allows the lighting process to become so much more fluid and experimental, that new horizons open up for the potential contribution of lighting to the performing arts.

The planning part of any lighting design process provides a palette. As long as each light requires manual adjustment, this palette will always be relatively inflexible. Because so much has to be planned in advance we have to play a little safe, going for something that we can be reasonably sure will work first time. And we are limited by our imagination. Admittedly, this is an imagination fed by all sorts of stimuli: text, music, pictures, rehearsals, past experiences etc. But the finest stimulation for working with light is experimenting with the light itself. Moving the beams, scrolling the colours – or even, as with Vari∗Lite, the mixing of virtually any colour coupled with instant diffusion and texturing of the beam – this is real painting. I have indicated some fears about dynamically moving beams. But this is an area with enormous dramatic possibilities:

- Shifting focus, boldly or delicately, from one part of the stage to another and from one actor to another.

- A moving beam that commands the eye of the audience to follow.

- A wide beam that narrows as the attention closes in on a solo actor.

- A narrow beam that gradually opens out to reveal an increasingly wide area.

- A series of moving beams that converge on one person.

- Slow start and dramatic acceleration.

- And, above all, doing this with the clean and continuous movement of a single beam rather than the sequential cross-fading of multiple beams.

But we must use this dynamic potential with some restraint, taking care to pace, contrast, hold back, finding the delicate balance between too much too soon and too little too late.

How about the interrelation of lighting *design* with lighting *management*? It has been suggested that the opportunity to experiment will lengthen the time taken by lighting sessions. Experience of memory desks over the past twenty years is that they have speeded up the lighting process, allowing much of the work that once required separate rehearsal time to be carried out simultaneously with actor rehearsals. There seems to be no reason why remote operation of luminaires should not be an extension of this. So we have the possibility of a great move forward in the efficiency of lighting management and the quality of lighting design. Practical success will depend on two major factors: the lights and the people who use them.

How about the lighting *instruments*? At this critical point in the development of remote-control, there must be a continuing debate between maker and user – an interaction between what is *possible* and what is *desirable*. It is not enough for manufacturers just to offer the possible, or the users just to demand the desirable, they must interact. And this interaction will, in particular, be concerned with establishing priorities. Reliability has to be at the top of any list. However, the new luminaries already seem to be well on the way to becoming sufficiently reliable, particularly in their repeat accuracy, to form the principal workhorses of our stage lighting installations.

Noise is a major development concern, although it is less of a problem in musicals than it is in drama. However, reliability must continue to be the overriding priority; I emphasise this because of history. We only need consider the situation which arose during the development of computer-based lighting desks: when most manufacturers listened too closely to the users (including me) who asked for more and more complex facilities. The result was a concentration on programming those extra facilities rather than *improving reliability*. So, perhaps, we need to start by establishing the minimum facilities required, rather than the maximum. I personally would prefer to have lots of instruments with basic functions under remote control rather than a small number of instruments that can do everything.

There will be a continuing need for both types of remote luminaire. The addition of motors to the controls of conventional spotlights – such as in the Strand PALS system – and the more radical approach using discharge lamps, mechanical shutter dimming, and internal dichroic colour mixing – in systems such as Vari*Lite.

Such remotely controlled lights may offer new possibilities, but the most fundamental aspect of light is the angle at which it strikes the actor or the scenic object. Does it come from above, from the side, or from the front and a little to the side? How much to the side? A very small change in the place where the light source is positioned will affect what we see. It is interesting to see that in many of the musicals where remote lights are used, the hardest-working lights are those capable of being moved from one position on the stage to another. Whatever sophisticated control we have over the beam size, shape, quality, and colour, the angle at which the beam hits actor or object is fixed by the position in which we mount the spotlight. Therefore, there is a limit to how far we can reduce the number of instruments, particularly in a permanent installation. So, increasingly, we are likely to see instruments travelling along trusses, propelled by motors taking instructions from the same digital control chain as the horizontal pan, the vertical tilt, and the focus. In my view, the facility enabling a light to track along a horizontal truss, or up and down a vertical tower, is much more important than having secondary adjustments such as remotely-controlled barndoors on a focus-spot or remotely operated shutters in a profile.

Vari*Lite has shown the degree of sophistication that is possible with a discharge profile, particularly control of texture by combining diffusion with gobos, and control of colour. The advantage of mixing dichroic filters within the instrument, rather than hanging a filter scroller on the front, is not just the number of colours available. Although scrolling through carefully chosen filters can be very dynamic and, at slow speeds, quite subtle, scrollers do not remove the need for using a pair of luminaires for crossfading from one colour to another. But microprocessed dichroics offer the possibility of very subtle programmed changes in the colour from a single lighting instrument.

The future looks exciting, but equipment development check-lists should include the following:

- How reliable is the engineering, particularly the repeat accuracy?

- How noisy? Not the noise of one new motor in a show-room, but many motors so intensively used that there is inadequate time available for maintenance.

- Do the luminaires have the adjustments we need?

- Are the controls sufficiently 'playable'?

- Will today's control be compatible with tomorrow's lights?

Check-lists for considering the *use* of this equipment should include:

- Will the new flexibility allow a reduction in the number of lights used? If so, by how much will this reduction be limited by that most critical feature of lighting design – the angle at which light strikes an actor or object?

- To what extent will the new technology require re-thinking of the way in which lighting is designed for stage productions?

The potential of light's contribution to the theatre experience seems poised for a major leap forward. But will we really succeed in harnessing this new technology to the service of theatre? Theatre is a *people* industry; consequently, success will depend upon the people who use these lights rather than the lights themselves. This, in turn, will depend to a large extent on the way we develop the education of all the visual workers in our theatres – not just the lighting specialists but the directors, choreographers and set designers. So it is important for the new technology to be installed in academies where directors, scenographers and lighting designers are educated.

There will be those who will say that this is wrong, declaring that students should first learn how to use basic equipment. Of course, they are right as far as learning about technology is concerned. But learning about light is about *experimenting* with light – experimenting with angles, with textures and with colours. It is about painting with light. With vastly improved access to such a palette we can, possibly for the first time, really start to teach lighting design.

I have concentrated to a large extent on moving lights because they are an area with tremendous potential for driving forward the art of lighting, yet also having the capability for creating havoc if we do not use them properly. But what about the normal lights, the ones that stand still until you go up a ladder? Traditional tungsten–halogen spotlights seem likely to remain the workhorse of most of our theatres, particularly simple plano–convex (PC) focus-spots. There will still be a role for lots of PARS – although improved lamp design could produce cleaner images, and there may perhaps be room for a slightly more sophisticated can. There are times when a longer can might be useful; many parcans are used as downlighters or as side crosslighters, so length is not quite the problem that it is with spots on bars lighting upstage or diagonally. A longer can might just contain more spill and keep the heat away from the filter. A rotating colour-frame could be useful with directional diffusers. There will always be a role for the traditional tungsten–halogen profile-spots and PC focus-spots. But with the improvements in PC lenses, the use of fresnels may decrease.

However, we may be near the end of the road for any significant developments of equipment based on conventional mains voltage tungsten lamps. The use of discharge lamps has been steadily increasing over the past twenty-five years and low-voltage lamps have long been an exciting source, particularly as exploited with parabolic reflectors in central Europe. However, the real potential for low voltage is the elusive model of electronic transformer that handles 500+ watts in a hostile environment and does not need a cooling fan. How long to go – ten years? Its arrival could signal all kinds of low-voltage spotlights, not just beamlights. Colour choice is becoming less agonising at the drawing board. Scrollers are established and Vari*Lite uses colour like paint. With dichroic mixing, filter numbers become irrelevant – just look at the stage as you mix.

Once upon a time I got very excited by controls. Now I have a very low threshold of boredom. When I go into a theatre, my question is not "What control do you have?" but "Who is the operator?" If an operator understands and likes their particular control, together we will rapidly achieve what I want in a hassle-free way. Good operators can extract anything out of the most unpromising control, so long as they know that control and, preferably, *like it*. The complexities of a control are for rehearsals. I personally have never yet succeeded in devising lighting that could not be operated, at performance, on the most basic memory control. But some of that lighting would have been very difficult to plot and would have taken for ever. But once we got memory – amnesia-free memory – and invented the wheel, we were there. So let the Wurlitzers roll, let the knobs flourish and multiply. Give the operators what they want but, boardmakers, beware those who sit down at your latest toy on an exhibition stand, determined just to find out what it will *not* do. We have been through a phase when 'me too' knobs tended to be given priority over system reliability and response speed. Analogue dimmers are dead for new installations; we now live in a multiplexed world of digital processing. These visions in the crystal ball could well turn out to be reasonably accurate for the next decade, because they are a purely an extension of what is already happening. But beyond that? Light is a waveform and as such it can be deflected and manipulated electronically. Must pan, tilt and focus be adjusted physically? Can this not be done electronically? If the visible light frequencies are inconvenient for electronic control, why not process at an intermediate frequency – between power input and light output? Perhaps we could shape the beam, colour it, diffuse it, even bend it, at a more amenable frequency before changing it to light? Why use colour filters? Can we not break-up the spectrum electronically? If we must continue to process energy at the frequency of light, shall we, perhaps, see something like liquid crystals taking over the shuttering, irising and even dimming – particularly of discharge sources?

But this is talk enough to crack any crystal ball. Whatever yet-to-be invented mechanisms the future holds as the means to realise lighting hopes and intentions, it will always be my personal conviction that the fewer instruments used in any particular cue, the cleaner the light will be.

The lighting designer's most important tool will remain the eraser. My best work has certainly been when I cut-back on the size of the rig. Some of these cut-back rigs have been very big, but I have tried to keep to clean visual statements. There may be seventy, or more, parcans alight but they are being used as a single instrument. In my youth, I was sometimes frustrated by the primitive technology. But we could usually make things happen, somehow. Of course, it took time because we had to adapt to the available technology and resort to tricks, (but theatre has always involved conjuring) whereas making it happen is now much easier.

What has not changed is the limitation of my imagination. The panic that all my visual ideas will be lousy ones and that my lighting will not integrate with the show. But technology is making it much easier and we must ensure that we continue to exploit technology to make the use of light easier – not as a staging peripheral but as an integral. Nothing on the stage exists until light reveals it and light is nothing until it hits something.

A postscript

Are *you* ready for a Cyberspace world? Do you welcome virtual reality or do you feel threatened by it? Unless you wish to remain in a twentieth-century timewarp, get measured for your sensor-laden bodysuit, electronic gloves and video goggles. It is time to "Walk through the computer-generated virtual reality that surrounds you, picking up and manipulating all the objects in this cyberspace world."

Designers often despair at the inability of directors to visualise how the model will scale-up to become a set. Despair no more. Director and designer can wear gloves and goggles and go walkabouts in the model; to rearrange the 'virtually real' as if it were virtually cardboard. Forget marking out rehearsal rooms, just dress the actors in the gear and let them get on with it in Cyberspace. Audience participation? It's not such a big step from handing out cardboard spectacles for a 3D movie. The ultimate in promenade performance – and with real audience participation. Out would go "It's behind yer!" to be replaced by "It's virtually around yer!" No need for lights or controls, just software.

To fear or embrace technology?

Theatre enjoys something of a love–hate relationship with its technology. We have all known moments when the simplicity of a few planks and a passion seemed infinitely more desirable than a hi-tech stage with the latest facilities which, wondrous though they may be, are increasingly complex to integrate, even when free from malfunction. Yet theatre technology is not exactly a new concept – earlier stage carpenters exploited their own century's knowledge of mechanical advantage to produce complex flying and scene-changing techniques that were not only labour-saving but could achieve a degree of sophisticated timing that now taxes the skills of a computer programmer. So why the fear? Perhaps it is fear of the unknown: the replacement of visible hardware with invisible software. Theatre people tend to be sensualists, responding to the touch of tangible objects. To pull a rope, push a flat, or turn a winch can be much more satisfying than initiating a programme by touching a button.

Theatre exists as soon as people are placed in an environment – they interact with each other and with that environment. These interactions can involve a complete range of sophistication from a soloist on a stool to a multimedia spectacular. Theatre exists in many forms, all valid within their own terms of reference. Many of these forms have always been dependent upon technology and will continue to seek ways of developing the desirable into the possible. Partly for humanity, in removing excessive physical drudgery, and partly for efficiency in releasing maximum time for rehearsal and performance – but primarily to explore ways of extending the nature of theatrical experience. Provided that we always seek the desirable rather than the merely possible, theatre has surely no alternative but to embrace technology.

To fear or embrace lighting design?

Theatre tends both to embrace and fear its lights and their designers. The embrace grows out of realisation that light is an essential constituent of a supportive stage environment. The fear has something of a rational basis arising from light being the very last ingredient to be added to the production mix. If the light falls short of expectations there is unlikely to be time available for anything but damage-limitation exercises. The only therapy is the mutual confidence that grows out of improved communication resulting from every theatre-person gaining an understanding of each other's specialism.

12
Am I Lit Here?

It is important that we resist any temptation to replace belief in the magic of theatre with cynicism about its people and processes. Theatre cynics damage theatre and ultimately destroy themselves. Nevertheless, personal survival does involve occasional cynical moments – but only as a valve to relieve an unsustainable build-up of individual or group tension. Many years ago, during one such personal moment, I shared some cynical thoughts with the readers of Tabs. Their sympathetic response left me in no doubt that I had struck chords in the angst which is generated by working in theatre lighting. The danger of cynicism is that it is has a core of truth. Indeed, sometimes it can be the most acceptable way to present truth in a palatable form. So, while cynicism is certainly a possible behavioural style, it should only be used, as should any particular lighting style, when appropriate and never become a doctrine.

My one unfulfilled ambition as a lighting designer is for an actor to break off in rehearsal and say "Don't you think there is just a little bit too much light on me here? Of course, it's fine for me personally but is it right for the atmosphere of the play?" My actors have certainly been known to favour me with little rehearsal speeches but the text is usually a variation on the theme 'Am I lit here?' These questions never take me by surprise because they are inevitably prefaced by much screwing-up of the actor's eyes accompanied by darting head-movements reminiscent of the mating dance of a Muscovy duck. I admit that an actor did, on one occasion, ask for less light, but the request was "Look, can you take down the light on me here – the !☆❂✳⊙!! author seems to have forgotten that I am in this scene!"

Very often, the only way to deal with the dark area down left is not by an increase of light on the left but by a reduction on the right. Only the bravest lighting designer would actually say this to an actor, although it is a sure way of finding out whether the director has much lighting experience. Rather than speak forth honestly and retire to lick their wounds, wise designers will merely say "Don't worry. I'm sorry that we have some balance problems, but I'm working on them." Then scribble furiously in your notebook. Whether you make an intelligible note will depend on your judgement of the situation, rather than that of the actor or director – eighty per cent of rehearsal notes are likely to be pure rhubarb.

To a large extent the art of lighting or, more accurately, the art of being a lighting designer, is not so much the handling of watts and lumens as the handling of people. By the nature of their calling, theatre-people in general, and actors in particular, are sensitive and analytical. Unfortunately, contemporary theatre has bred some directors who prey on the sensitivity of actors and turn self-analysis into a wounding self-criticism which produces feelings of inadequacy.

The better directors work by building the self-confidence of their actors and production teams. They keep their cool, smiling and encouraging. But, perhaps most important of all, they accept blame and admit mistakes (even when they know it is not their fault) in order to keep the production flowing smoothly forwards. They make constructive use of psychology to build the actors and production team into a happy and harmonious unit. Such positive use of psychology makes more sense than using it destructively – to impose personal concepts on an unhappy cast and production team who are then only able to respond with a professional competence lacking the essential support of a committed belief. It is the duty of we light-persons to try to use psychology in a positive way. We normally learn the hard way. Or at any rate I did – and do.

Some years ago, I had to transfer a long-running play from one London theatre to another. The second theatre – although having much better auditorium lighting positions – had a shallower stage so that the scenery had to be set tight to the proscenium, leaving no space for perch lighting booms. The star lady spent a long part of the play seated at a table facing the perch and over the months had become accustomed to the glare in her eyes, although she was not particularly well lit. In the second theatre, the auditorium box boom-position produced a much better lighting angle but the lights did not shine in her eyes. The inevitable happened: speeches on the theme of 'Am I lit here?' soon escalated via "Well, if there is light here I am having trouble finding it!" to "Well, if I am expected to play this scene in a blackout…" In vain I (and the director, bless him!) tried explain the situation. "A float spot," she cried, "if we cannot have perches let's have a float spot."

And then I leaped in with both feet: "A float (footlight) spot would make distorted shadows of you on the ceiling and these would distract the audience so that they looked at the shadows instead of at you." There was a pause while she drew herself up to her full 5ft 2 ¼ inches. "Darling," she declared icily, "I think you will find that when I am on, the audience will look only at *me*." So, the very next morning, a spot went into the floats, the lens was removed, diffuser inserted and the 100 watt bulb run at twenty per cent on the dimmer. It was not an effective light source, but she could gaze into it while seated at her table. I am told that I took the resultant 'I told you so' speech very well.

Floats are a key item in the affairs of the lighting psychologist. To audiences they are traditionally the primary source of stage lighting and to actors they are a source of comfort. Actors do seem to get quite a confidence boost from floats. Often, this takes the form of a rather ill-defined warmth; although one famed comedy actress told me that she loved floats as a friendly protection against her audience who she described as "…those devouring monsters out there." On the other hand this particular lady always establishes an immediate contact with her audience – a contact which is more immediate and more intense than the contact achieved by some theorists who profess to love their audience and leap about on thrust stages but fail to project their performance beyond the third row.

As actors are so aware of floats and they are of little value as a positive lighting source, it can be a good place to pander to their colour prejudices. Actresses over a certain age are liable to become mentally unhinged at the mere thought of amber light and in the more extreme cases they are likely to regard even a delicate gold tint as an amber, so do I ever put an amber in the floats? Pale lavenders can be rather more difficult. "Ah!, so you are the lighting designer," – spoken in a whisper – "I need lots of help from you." – unconvincing gestures of protest from me. "Now, I hope we are going to have lots of that lovely surprise-pink", or "We are not going to have any of that nasty surprise-pink nonsense, are we, darling?"

Whatever she wants, the place to put it is in the floats – the only place that she will notice it (writing the number in jumbo letters on the filter helps). I have had plays starring both these ladies and in choosing which one to play off against the other, I remember that in such circumstances the word *darling* is not used as a term of endearment but as a threat. I had to use floats once (a circuit of blue at half-check) in a five-roomed multiple set to help an ageing actress find the audience – I do admit to that being a rather abnormal use of a lighting source. More fundamental is the use of the floats to house comic's props: a random check at a recent pantomime found that the front of the stage was harbouring (in addition to 5 microphones, 4 UV tubes, 3 flash-boxes and 2 strobes) a fishing rod, a pair of pistols, an aerosol foghorn and a packet of instant whip. Since the theatre in question had no footlights, a dummy timber masking piece had to be placed along the front of the stage.

Where floats are of no value whatsoever is in the treatment of the white-light syndrome. This disease is normally accompanied by side-effects which take the form of prejudices against anything that could be considered, however remotely, as 'traditional'. Common causes are fear of colour or fear of lighting designers. Sufferers have been known to grow out of it, but the only real cure is to be forced to do a commercial 'drinks table behind the sofa' comedy under the supervision of what is known on Broadway as a 'participating *prodoocer*'.

In fact, the tragedy of white-lighting people is that instead of regarding white as *one* possible lighting style they think of it as the *only* style – whereas an open-minded light designer will aim to identify an appropriate lighting style within the overall style of each individual production. Conversations with the director in pursuit of this aim often produce a lot of literary rhubarb which boils down to a suspicion that everyone is going to act 'sort of normal'. "Ah!," you say, tugging your beard – a more useful prop to a lighting designer than an extra spot-bar – "barely-heightened realism?" The director looks grateful and, if you have succeeded in gaining his confidence, within minutes will be using the phrase to the actors in rehearsal.

In practice, there are four basic lighting styles to fall back on: Rosy Cosy Glow, Operatic Steel, Shady Mud and Single Source Bashit.

- **Rosy Cosy Glow** is a smooth, general coverage in warm tones, usually with some attempt at sculptural quality. Its usefulness lies in the cosy credibility which it gives to fading scenery and fading performances.

- **Operatic Steel** favours extensive side-lighting to disguise the facial contortions that accompany the production of sustained vocal tone. It is noticed by music critics who call it imaginative; it certainly is dramatic and therefore particularly favoured by those operatic directors to whom the music is an undramatic intrusion.

- **Shady Mud** is defended by declarations about the theatrical power of light and shade, but its supporters rarely differentiate between planned and random darkness. Lights tend to be focused for the benefit of floor rather than face, but there are enough of them to create sufficient bounce to throw up a rather indiscriminate illumination, given the texture of mud by indecisive filtering of excessively-dimmed sources.

- **Single Source Bashit** is favoured by puritans and by repentant shady-mudders unwilling to master the craft of smoothly overlapped focusing. Theory says that if natural light comes from one big sun, or one big moon, stage light should come from one big lamp; practice proves that the reflected light which may be fine for a room is unlikely to be enough for a theatre – ask any comedian.

I am sorry if all this seems to have a stylistic flavour of barely-heightened *cynicism*, but it is necessary for well-balanced lighting designers to note and analyse such matters if they are to keep their cool in the face of such tragi–comedy situations as 'The great Broadway musical myth'. Musical production teams tend to work by trial and error in an atmosphere of studied hysteria. Life becomes a continuous day and night conference where the dialogue has all the studied flatness of a space mission and the most frequent phrase is "We have a problem." Every piece of the show is re-written, re-orchestrated, re-choreographed, re-costumed and re-directed several times, gradually getting worse and worse. Finally, when all else has failed, the entire production team round on the lighting designer to announce that "What this show needs is more dynamic lighting."

At this point, the psychologically orientated lighting designer must not say "Look, I know the lighting is bad but it is no worse than the rest of the show." No, just tug at your beard (real or metaphorical) and swing into the re-light. This should commence with an hour's feverish activity to change colours – nothing very drastic, just a few of the more extreme colours into lights which were not doing very much anyway. Having quietly cautioned the board operator not to lose the original plot, go through the show, cue-by-cue, doing some dynamic alterations like changing cyclorama colours and reducing the odd full-up to a couple of splashes of magenta and green. The production team will be temporarily enthusiastic, the actors less so. It will cost a lot of money in overtime (none, unfortunately, for you as the lighting designer) and during the next few days you will slowly move back to the original light-plot which may not be dynamic but at least you can see the actors.

In the final analysis, being a lighting designer is really a matter of inspiring *confidence*. The difficulty in doing this is that the lighting designer is the last of the production team to make a contribution. The value of the actors, of the costumes, of the sound can begin to be assessed at relatively early stages in rehearsals but until the very last days lighting designers can only produce diagrammatic plans to back-up their expensive estimates.

Who can blame the director for a nagging fear that if the lighting designer's contribution is ghastly it will be too late to do anything about it.

Wise lighting designers keep popping into rehearsals, remembering that the frequency of visits is more important than their length. They also distribute lots of copies of the lighting plan, remembering that immaculate draughtsmanship often arouses suspicion. When you get into the theatre, remember that lighting designers, because they do their bit last, are expected to make up all the time lost by the other technical departments. Mention it, accept it, but do not shout about it.

As you prepare to plot the cues, expect the set designer to want the opposite to the director. There are three possible situations: first, when director and set designer are in total harmony over their conception. Secondly, when the director wants the action shadowy and the set designer would like to see every set detail exposed. Thirdly, when the director wants the actors bathed in a great bash of light but the designer would like the set clothed in atmospheric gloom. The second and third situations are the more common and it is the fate of the lighting designer to devise the necessary compromise – a decision which is not simplified by advice from the assorted committee of self-declared 'experts' who appear, seemingly by magic, at the mere suggestion of a lighting rehearsal. To the lighting designer, I can recommend one effective if unpleasant remedy: chicken pox. I once sat lighting in the stalls of the vast Liverpool Empire with this infectious disease while my supporting committee retreated to the grand circle. The braver members occasionally shouted advice from their heavenly heights but it did not penetrate my temperature-induced haze. An effective ploy, but drastic and lacking the subtlety of the true lighting psychologist.

Epilogue

In every theatre, waiting in the wings, ever ready to leap on stage at the drop of a crystal ball, there is a *soothsayer*. Whatever their cue, the response is the same: "Woe, woe and thrice woe." Hardly surprising perhaps, for is not theatre supposed to hold a mirror up to nature, and do we not live in a world where doomsday is just around the corner, with banner headlines screaming disaster predictions and pundits offering woe in philosopher's clothing? We live in a world where no news is good news and good news is no news. The media, when pressed, protest that they are our servants and so they tell us what we want to hear.

It therefore takes some courage to look in the crystal ball to soothsay the future and find a cheerful prospect. Nevertheless, I offer the view that theatre in general – and lighting in particular – are now generally far better than before. While we could be on pinnacle poised for slippery descent, destiny is surely a matter for positive control rather than woeful soothsaying.

There is only one thing that can really go wrong with theatre and that is a *failure to communicate with the audience*. If I have any woeful warning to sound, it is that I think I detect an occasional tendency to forget, ignore, and even despise, the audience who are the *reason* for theatre. However, the point has not yet been reached where it is necessary to sound the clarion call for an audience-liberation movement.

All the required positive action is contained within the First Law of Theatre which states: 'When in doubt, up a point'. In terms of lighting, the point is a literal one: the ten-per-cent point on a dimmer scale. But the point is also a metaphor for making everything just a touch bigger, broader, brighter and louder. The audience do not have our knowledge of the play. Weeks of reading, discussing and rehearsing make us receptive to every nuance. But to most of the audience it is all new. They have a lot to absorb in a short time, starting with who's who. An audience has to be won over, especially those who are there to keep their companions happy. The subtleties are clear to us but will these subtleties be clear to them? If in any doubt, up a point!

Glossary

Analogue   Traditional processing and transmission of information as a continuous electrical signal – see *Digital*.

Angle   The angle at which light hits an actor or element of scenery.

Argand lamp   A bright and steady light provided by the circular flame from a circular wick (for oil) or burner (for gas), protected from draught by a glass chimney,

Assistant Stage Manager (ASM)   Junior member of the stage management team. During light-plotting sessions, often stands in actor positions to help intensity adjustments.

Autocad   A computer-aided design (CAD) program which is used by many theatre organisations for drawing stage plans. In conjunction with software such as *Modelbox Autolight*, it can be used for computer-aided lighting design.

Board   Contraction of switchboard or dimmerboard, still used to describe lighting-control desks, although these have become highly sophisticated information-processing centres.

Beamlights   Lensless instruments with a parabolic reflector giving a near-parallel beam.

Birdie   Tiny low-voltage spotlight, fed by an external transformer.

Cans Headsets with microphone and single earpiece, used by technicians for communication between each other and with the stage manager who calls the cues.

Channels The paths from the operator's finger on the control desk through all the processing to the dimmers and onwards to the sockets into which lights have been plugged. On most modern boards, a channel can control several dimmers, if desired. Thus, the number of channels is effectively the number of independent 'brush strokes' in the 'light palette'.

Check A decrease in light intensity.

Colour call A listing of the colour filters required for each instrument on the lighting design plan.

Control desk see *Board*.

Crossfade A lighting cue where the current state (picture) is replaced by a different one, with some channels decreasing or increasing their intensity while others may remain unchanged.

Cue Strictly speaking the signal which initiates any change on stage, although often used to refer to the change itself.

Deputy Stage Manager (DSM) The member of the stage management team, in the British theatre, who integrates all the departmental contributions to a performance by calling the cues.

Digital Processing and transmitting information by a sequence of distinct but infinitesimally-short bits, rather than as a continuous signal – see *Analogue*.

Digitiser A control surface which enables information to be converted into digital form for microprocessing.

Dimmer   Devices which, in response to information from the control desk, change light intensity by varying the electricity supply to the lamp.

Director   The leader of the production team with ultimate responsibility for realising a script from conception through to performance. Has dictatorship powers, although good directors are seldom seen using them.

Dress rehearsals   The final rehearsals, run as if performances, with every technical facility in operation, and only stopped in the event of a major problem which results in total loss of continuity.

Electro-magnetic   Prior to solid-state thyristor-based dimming, remote control usually involved driving the moving parts of all the dimmers from a common motorised shaft, with each dimmer having a pair of magnetic clutches, one to raise, the other to dim.

Enter   The key on a computer keyboard which instigates an action that has been selected by using the other keys. North American lighting-control philosophy favours the use of an Enter key to activate any selected action whereas in Europe all selected actions are immediate.

Fibre optics   Fine glass-fibres which transmit light. The ends of the fibre provide the finest available points of light, making them particularly suitable for stars on a backcloth.

Filter   Plastic material used to diffuse or colour the light by removing parts of the spectrum to enhance the effect of the remaining spectral components.

Flare   Unwanted light reflected from scenery or the front parts of spotlights, particularly barndoors.

Focusing	Adjusting an instrument's pan and tilt, together with the beam size, shape and quality, to light the required part of stage.
Focus-spot	Simple spotlight which controls the width of its conical beam by moving lens and reflector towards (wider) and away from (narrower) a fixed lens.
Follow-spots	Spotlights with operators who keep them focused on the actors as they move around the stage – see *Limes*.
Fresnel	A lens where the front surface is stepped and the rear dimpled to give a very soft, diffused light. This diffusion generates some scatter of light close to the lens and can be a problem when these lights hang close to scenery.
FOH	All the lighting instruments which are 'Front of House', that is on the auditorium side of the proscenium.
Group	Several channels selected for control by one master.
HMI	A type of high-powered discharge lamp.
Instrument	General term for all stage lighting units – whether floodlight, spotlight or beamlight – which house a source and have facilities for panning, tilting, focusing etc.
Iris	Adjustable circular diaphragm. Placed in the gate of a profile-spot, particularly when used as a follow-spot, to vary the size of the gate and therefore the size of a circular beam. The muscular iris in the human eye is a protective device which adjusts the aperture to varying light intensities.
Light pen	A device which provides immediate access to a

channel or control facility by touching a video screen or a *magic sheet* (qv) on a *digitiser* (qv).

Limes Jargon for follow-spots and their operators, dating from when follow-spots were limelights in which an oxy–hydrogen flame made a block of lime brilliantly incandescent.

Linnebach A method of projecting scenery by casting a shadow of a large profiled 'slide'.

Load The electrical power, in kilowatts, of the lights assigned to a dimmer and limited by the rating of that dimmer.

Magic sheet A small simplified plan providing easy reference to channel numbers. Computer versions use a digitiser (qv) to enable direct-channel access by touching the symbols on the plan.

Master A lever or push which activates a group, preset or memory.

Multicore Cable sheath enclosing individual wires for several circuits. Now used mainly for feeding spot-bars. Control systems formerly required multicores with a separate wire to carry the control voltage for each channel, but multiplex time-sharing now allows all information to be carried digitally along a single wire.

Multipreset Manual boards with duplicated or triplicated sets of channel levers to allow the levels for complete subsequent cue states to be set up in advance.

Optical effects Moving pictorial images of clouds, fire, water, rain, snow, etc., generated by replacing the stationary slide in a projection system with a motor-driven rotating glass disc.

Parcan　Simple lighting instrument, producing an intense near-parallel beam, using a par lamp which includes a fixed optical system within the lamp envelope.

Patching　Allocating lights to dimmers by means of a centralised plug-and-socket system resembling a manual telephone exchange.

Piano board　Portable resistance dimmerboards, common in the United States and standard in Broadway prior to the introduction of computerised memory systems.

Plot　List of all preparations and actions required during a performance. Board plots for manual systems required the level of every channel, in every cue, to be written down, whereas plots for memory systems need note only the file numbers and master keystroke actions.

Profile-spots　Spotlights which project a hard or soft profile of any two-dimensional shape such as shutters, iris or gobo, placed at the centre ('gate') of the optical system. Most profile-spots have a pair of lenses with independent movement allowing a wide range of beam angles with the option of soft or hard edge.

Remainder dim　A control board keystroke used during focusing. It keeps the last selected channel alive while fading any other channels to blackout.

Rig　An installation of lighting instruments positioned for a production. To 'rig' is the process of hanging these lights in position.

Scatter　Stray light outside the main beam, particularly from a fresnel lens.

Scenographer　International word for set designer. It implies scenery used as an integrated environment rather than a decorative background.

Scroller Colour-changer where colours are selected by a computer-generated signal from a series of filters taped together and driven by an extremely fast motor.

Soft patching The processors of most boards now allow any dimmer or dimmers to be allocated to any channel.

State The lighting picture arrived at after a cue.

Technical rehearsal A slow, stopping rehearsal which integrates the actors with set, costumes, lights, sound and all technological aspects of the stage environment.

Thyristor The standard solid-state (no moving parts) dimmer.

VDU (Video Display Unit) Monitor screen on which all cue information can be displayed, particularly the levels of each channel in each memory.